LAW OF THE LAND

A Practical Legal Guide for Tourists and Business Travelers

Mexico

By Michael L. Moore Esq.

DEDICATION

This book is dedicated to the memory of my late older brother, Kenneth Lee Moore, whose tragic murder at 15 years of age, inspired me to write these series of books.

This book is also dedicated to my parents, John Henry Moore, and Edna Mae Moore, whose tremendous parenting skills kept me focused on the important things in life, ... being reverent, getting educated, and prioritizing family.

Finally, this book is dedicated to my Beautiful family, my wife Royellen, my son AJ, and my daughter Karla. They inspire me every single day to be kind, patient, and compassionate.

IN LOVING MEMORY OF:

Belinda Joyce Moore Moss—My Beautiful and Wonderful Sister who supported me in every positive thing that I ever attempted to do.

Michael Eugene Baker—My Dedicated and Loyal Friend and Brother who always wanted the very Best for me.

Sylvia Joyce Hill—my eldest sister, who had a beautiful spirit and was like a second mother to me.

LAW OF THE LAND®

PUBLISHING for Tourists & Business Travelers

Travel smart. Stay legal. Stay safe.®

From local laws to medical guides we've got you covered world wide
in one digital platform.

PREFACE

My introduction to the justice system came when I was only 10 years old. My 15-year-old brother was murdered with a butcher knife by a 19-year-old in a simple argument over a torn shirt. I was devastated by his death and sought retribution for his fate that never came. The woman was initially charged with second degree murder, but after plea negotiations, she was convicted of manslaughter and sentenced to only five years in a youthful offender school and ordered to undergo psychiatric care. That was it. Nothing more. The judicial system had run its course.

My family knew nothing about the justice system, and we did not have the tools to advocate for ourselves. No one provided us with a written source to reference for guidance through this process. There was no easily accessible, easy to understand, definitive source to use to educate ourselves about the legal system that we suddenly and unexpectedly found ourselves immersed in after being victimized by such a violent criminal act.

As I got older, finished college, law school, and ultimately started practicing law, it became clear to me that most people are not knowledgeable about the law or how the judicial process works. If most people are uninformed here in the United States regarding the law and the legal process, how would they fare when in other countries? I realized that tourists and businesspeople who travel internationally needed access to information on how to navigate the legal system in other countries!

For many years, there has been considerable media attention focused on international travelers experiencing legal difficulties while traveling abroad. Most of these news stories gained attention in the United States and abroad because they involved American citizens facing punishment that was considered "unconventional" and "harsh" by United States' legal standards. I recall a news story in 1994 regarding Michael Fay, a young American male, who had broken the law in Singapore. He was convicted and sentenced to be caned and or whipped publicly. While the United States Government weighed in on the inappropriate and cruel nature of the punishment, the young American was beaten because he had been convicted under Singapore law.

Similarly, in recent years, international news stories have garnered headlines regarding foreign travelers and their issues with the laws of countries that were not their own. Amanda Knox, an American woman, was accused of murdering her roommate in Italy in 2007 and spent almost four years in an Italian prison before being definitively acquitted by the Supreme Court of Cassatio. Kenneth Bae, an American citizen, was arrested in North Korea in 2012 and was convicted for hostile acts against the communist country. He was sentenced to 15 years hard labor but was released in 2014 after efforts by the U.S. State Department. More recently, United States Basketball Star, Brittany Griner was arrested in February 2022 at a Moscow airport on drug-related charges and detained for nearly 10 months, spending much of that time in prison. Her plight unfolded at the same time Russia invaded Ukraine and further heightened tensions between Russia and the United States, ending only after she was freed in exchange for a notorious Russian arms dealer.

It was in 1994 that another personal tragic event occurred that also inspired me to write these series of books. A dear friend and client of mine was brutally murdered while on his second honeymoon in Jamaica. News of his murder shocked me and our local community. The legal hurdles his family had to overcome to see that justice was properly dispensed far away from home, in another country, with an entirely different set of criminal procedural rules and laws, was difficult to navigate.

As I was my friend's attorney at the time of his death, his family asked that I act as their "legal liaison" to the Jamaican Prosecutor's Office and to the Jamaican Police Department. I participated in multiple police interviews with my client's widow because she was the primary witness to his murder. As a former prosecuting attorney, I was also allowed by the Court, as a professional courtesy, to sit at the prosecutor's table to consult with the prosecuting attorney during trial. What I observed about the Jamaican trial process from a front row seat was compelling enough to cause me to seriously consider educating the "world" regarding what to expect and how to act appropriately when faced with legal issues while traveling abroad.

One of the realities in life is that, regardless of what country you are in, it is never a pleasant experience to run afoul of the law and be forced to accept that someone else will be making a decision about your pecuniary, proprietary, or penal interests (your money, your property, or your freedom).

It is important to know what the laws are, how they apply to you, and how to navigate the legal system if you are charged with a crime. It is also very helpful to know what resources are available to you if you are the victim of a criminal act. At the end of the day, an "ounce of prevention is worth a pound of cure," so the more knowledge you have, the more ammunition you possess, and the more likely you will have a positive outcome.

If you are traveling to Mexico, the first thing you should pack is a copy of this book! The helpful information and tips contained in this volume will provide a great starting point for knowing what to do (and not to do!) when you arrive at your destination, and will help ensure that you have a wonderful vacation or business trip unmarred by tangles with the law.

TABLE OF CONTENTS

INTRODUCTION

INTRODUCTION

As a practicing attorney for over 34 years, I have represented numerous clients who travel often, but are unaware of the laws of the land they are traveling to.

Therefore, many years ago, I decided to write a series of books that would explain the laws of specific countries. My focus was to explain the laws that may affect travelers in a straightforward manner, without all of the legal language that is sometimes hard for even seasoned attorneys to understand.

About This Book

The aim of this book is simple: it provides you, the traveler, with a simple, easy to read book that will provide a basic legal guide that explains the law in the country that you are about to visit. It is not intended to educate you on ALL of the laws in a given country, the goal is to provide you with the details of the most common legal and safety issues faced by tourists and business travelers.

I have also provided context with background information on places not to visit, statistics on the country as well as prevention measures you should take to safeguard your legal and physical safety. Knowledge is a powerful thing and knowing how to stay out of trouble (or how to get out of it!) is important for everyone who travels.

This *Law of The Land/Mexico* book simply helps you become more informed about your legal rights, responsibilities, and obligations in a wide range of subject areas.

Last, but not least, this book does NOT purport to offer legal advice. It does, however, provide the information you need to stay safe, follow the law and how to navigate around legal difficulties. However, if you do face legal difficulties, the information in this book will provide you with a starting point for solving the problem and obtaining legal assistance should it be required.

Hypotheticals Used Throughout This Book

From time to time throughout this book, I will explain the law to readers by using hypothetical scenarios. These hypotheticals will be marked by an icon that will be explained in further detail as you read on.

How This Book is Organized

CHAPTER 1: **About Mexico.** This chapter will provide you with a brief overview about Mexico and its history. It also addresses the best way to travel to Mexico, visa requirements, monetary advice, and the best times to visit.

CHAPTER 2: **Customs.** This chapter will provide information on what to expect when entering Mexico and documentation that is required. It will also explain what restricted and prohibited items are when entering Mexico along with what must be declared when returning to your destination from Mexico.

CHAPTER 3: **Crime in Mexico.** This chapter provides an overview of the history of crime in Mexico and steps that Mexican officials have taken to curb the high rate of crime.

CHAPTER 4: **Criminal Law Violations.** This chapter will provide information on drug offenses, primarily marijuana and cannabis products, penalties, and questions and answers about marijuana.

CHAPTER 5: **Alcohol-Related Offenses.** This chapter will provide key points regarding the sale, consumption, and regulations of alcohol use in Mexico.

CHAPTER 6: **Firearm & Ammunition Offenses.** This chapter will provide key points regarding the possession of firearms and ammunition in Mexico.

CHAPTER 7: **Prostitution.** This chapter provides an overview of the history of prostitution in Mexico, laws and penalties, prostitution practices, sex trafficking, sex tourism, and health in Mexico, tips to avoid being hassled, a Law of the Land Hypothetical and the current situation on prostitution in Mexico.

CHAPTER 8: **LGBTQ.** This chapter will provide information regarding the acceptance of LGBTQ people in Mexico, and the laws surrounding homosexuality.

CHAPTER 9: **Sexually Motivated/ Violent Crimes.** This chapter will provide an overview of sexually related crimes in Mexico.

CHAPTER 10: **Arrested in Mexico.** This chapter will provide information on what to do if you are arrested in Mexico.

CHAPTER 11: **Jails vs. Prisons: Conditions & Culture.** This chapter will provide information on the conditions and culture of Mexican jails and prisons.

CHAPTER 12: **Helping a Friend or Relative Imprisoned in Mexico.** This chapter will provide information on how you can assist a friend or relative imprisoned in Mexico.

CHAPTER 13: **The Administration of Justice.** This chapter will provide information on Mexico's judicial system.

CHAPTER 14: **Crime Victim Assistance.** This chapter will provide information on crime victim assistance along with providing safety tips.

CHAPTER 15: Police. This chapter will provide information on the Mexican Police and how to report a crime.

CHAPTER 16: How to Get Legal Help in Mexico. This chapter will provide information regarding how to obtain legal assistance for travelers to Mexico.

CHAPTER 17: Medical Facilities & Hospitals. This chapter will provide information about how to obtain medical care while visiting Mexico.

CHAPTER 18: Driving in Mexico. This chapter will provide information on driving in Mexico, its traffic rules, and road safety tips.

CHAPTER 19: Nude Beaches and Clothing-Optional Resorts. This chapter will provide an overview of nude beaches in Mexico, and the legality and safety of visiting nude beaches in Mexico.

CHAPTER 20: Unusual Laws. This chapter will provide information on some unusual laws in Mexico, and penalties and fines.

CHAPTER 21: Traveling Safely. This chapter will provide information on women traveling alone, crime prevention for families, safety notes for all travelers, and overall advice.

CHAPTER 22: Tourist Taxation. This chapter will provide information on taxes that tourists are required to pay in Mexico.

CHAPTER 23: Long-Term Stays. This chapter will provide an overview of the consequences for overstaying your visit to Mexico.

CHAPTER 24: Civil Litigation. This chapter will provide information about the civil litigation process in Mexico.

CHAPTER 25: Other Things to Know. This chapter will provide information on the harassment of tourists, travel and safety, and other practical tips.

CHAPTER 26: **Quick Reference Guide.** This chapter is a quick way to get information. It is a condensed version of the chapters in this book.

Emergency/Important Contact Numbers in Mexico

Useful Spanish Phrases

Glossary

Icons Used in this Book

What do those pictures throughout the book mean? See below:

WARNING: This icon flags information about things you should avoid while visiting Mexico. Heed the advice next to this icon to avoid legal perils.

REMEMBER: This icon flags noteworthy information that you shouldn't forget.

HELPFUL TIPS: This icon flags information that will help you when entering Mexico, relates to a legal situation, or refers to resources available while visiting Mexico.

TECHNICAL INFORMATION: This icon flags technical aspects of the law. If you are faced with a legal problem, and you want to learn more about the law involved, this information can be helpful.

 **ADDITIONAL INFORMATION**: This icon points to the location of additional information available on the internet.

 **HYPOTHETICAL**: This icon points to hypothetical scenarios to illustrate possible legal problems and the outcome.

 **QUESTIONS**: This icon points to questions and answers throughout the book.

 **TRUE STORY**: This icon points to true events throughout the book.

Where to Go From Here

If you have a specific question about the law in Mexico as it relates to a specific area, just turn to the chapter that addresses that issue or turn to the Quick Reference Guide.

You can also read this book from cover to cover to obtain a more comprehensive understanding of the Mexican laws and resources available should you find yourself in a legal predicament while visiting.

 **Disclaimer:** While the recommendations in this book primarily address U.S. citizens, the information is relevant and applicable to citizens of any country.

ABOUT MEXICO

ABOUT MEXICO

About Mexico

Mexico is located in the southern part of North America, bordering the United States to the north, and Guatemala and Belize to the southeast. It is the third largest country in Latin America and the 13th largest country in the world by area! Mexico is the 10th most populated country in the world, with a population of almost 130 million, known for its warm climate, dreamy beaches, rainforests and deserts, ancient ruins, colorful culture and remarkable cuisine.

Mexico won its independence from Spain in 1821, and September 16th is celebrated as the Mexican Independence Day. Mexico is a federal republic, with the president as the head of state and government. It has a free market economy and is a member of the North American Free Trade Agreement (NAFTA). It has a dynamic industrial base, vast mineral resources, and a wide-ranging service sector. As its official name suggests, the Estados Unidos Mexicanos (United Mexican States) incorporates 31 socially and physically diverse states and Mexico City, the Federal District.

It's capital, Mexico City, is one of the world's most important cities for business, culture, and education'. In fact, Forbes Magazine considers it the "number one world destination for business travelers."[1]

---

1   https://www.forbes.com/sites/nathanielparishflannery/2023/11/29/why-is-mexico-city-the-worlds-number-one-destination-to-visit/

Mexico City is the longest city in the world, stretching 200 kilometers (124.27 miles) from north to south, and is the most populous city in North America, with a population of over 9 million people. It is also one of the world's fastest-growing metropolitan areas and generates about one-third of Mexico's industrial production.

Mexico's population is composed of many ethnic groups, including indigenous peoples, Mexicans of European heritage, and mestizos (a result of the blending of indigenous and European peoples). Mexico is also home to a large number of expatriates, having the largest American expat community in the world.

There are 291 languages spoken in Mexico, the top 3 Nahuatl, Yucatec Maya and Spanish are, spoken by roughly 94% of the population.

The predominant religion in Mexico is Christianity, with the largest denomination being Roman Catholicism. According to the 2020 Mexican government census, about 78% of the population identifies as Roman Catholic while about 10% of the population is Protestant. Other religious groups include Judaism, Jehovah's Witnesses, and The Church of Jesus Christ of Latter-day Saints (about 1.5%), whereas 8.1% of the population claims no religion. A small fraction of Indigenous people in Mexico practice syncretic religions, which combine Catholicism with Indigenous beliefs.

Mexico is a relatively inexpensive destination to visit and can be very budget-friendly. However, some top tourist destinations (such as Mexico City, Los Cabos, and Cancun) are becoming more expensive. It also depends on what time of year you travel. During high season (December through April), with the busiest periods being Christmas and Easter, crowds are larger and prices are higher. Hotel rates can be double what they are during low season (June to mid-October). If you're planning to travel during high season, you should book as far in advance as possible!

Mexico, the Basics

How to get there?

The easiest way to travel to Mexico is to fly. Mexico is well-connected internationally, with several major airports serving as gateways to the country. Some of the biggest airports include:

- Mexico City International Airport (MEX)
- Cancún International Airport (CUN)
- Los Cabos International Airport (SJD)
- Guadalajara International Airport (GDL)
- Monterrey International Airport (MTY)

Big airlines such as Aeroméxico, American Airlines, Delta, United Airlines, Interjet, British Airways and more. All have several flights to Mexico. The cheapest times to visit Mexico are typically during the shoulder seasons (between the peak and offseason), April to June and September to November, avoiding peak holidays and considering mid-week travel.

When to visit?

The best time to visit Mexico depends on what you want to do and where you want to go:

Weather

The best weather is usually between December and April, when it's dry and warm. However, the weather varies by region:

- **NORTH**: The desert north is very dry, with temperatures reaching 100°F in the summer.
- **CENTER**: Mexico City and the central regions have a moderate climate, with daytime temperatures rarely dropping below 59°F.

- **COAST**: Coastal resort towns are best from November to April, when the weather is dry and warm with cool nights.

Crowds

The most popular time to visit is December to April, so if you want to avoid crowds, you can try May or June.

Festivals

Mexico has many festivals, including Carnaval in February, Día de los Muertos in early November, and Mexican Independence Day on September 15 and 16.

Activities

- **WHALE WATCHING**: February to March is a good time to see whales in Baja California.
- **DIVING AND SNORKELING**: The summer is a good time to dive or snorkel the coral reefs.
- **HIKING**: March is a good time to hike in the canyons.
- **SURFING**: May to August are good times for surfing.

Do I Need a Visa?

You DO NOT need a visa for Mexico if you meet the following conditions:

- You're visiting for tourism, business, transit, technical activities, or as a journalist or student.
- Your stay is less than 180 days.
- You won't earn any money in Mexico.
- You have a valid, multiple entry visa or permanent residence permit from the United States, Canada, Japan, the United Kingdom, or Schengen countries.

- You're visiting a Mexican maritime port by cruise.
- You're a national of Ukraine, Russia, or Turkey.
- You have an APEC (Asia – Pacific Economic Cooperation) Business Travel Card-ABTC.

If you're not eligible for a visa exemption, you can apply for a Mexican visa by booking an appointment through the MiConsulado (MyConsulate) booking system. You'll need to bring your passport, visa application form, and all supporting documents to the Mexican Embassy on the day of your appointment.

You should also make sure your passport is valid for at least six months from the date of your intended trip to Mexico.

How to Get Around?

Mexico offers a wide variety of transportation options to suit different budgets and preferences. Whether you're traveling within a city, exploring the countryside, or visiting coastal regions, here's a guide on how to navigate the country:

1. Public Transportation

- **BUSES**: Intercity buses (*autobuses*) like ADO connect major cities. For local trips, *camiones* and *microbuses* are affordable but may be confusing for visitors.
- **METRO**: In cities like Mexico City, the metro is cheap and efficient, though crowded during rush hours.
- **TAXIS AND RIDESHARING**: Official taxis can be hailed, but apps like Uber and DiDi are safer and more convenient in major cities.

2. Rental Cars

Renting a car is ideal for exploring outside cities. Companies like Hertz and Avis operate in most locations, but city driving can be chaotic. Be prepared for tolls on highways.

3. Bikes and Scooters

- **BIKE-SHARING**: Programs like Ecobici (Mexico City) are affordable.
- **ELECTRIC SCOOTERS**: Companies like Lime offer rentals via an app, which is great for short trips.

4. Ferries and Boats

For coastal areas or islands (like Cozumel), ferries are common, and private water taxis are available in some beach towns.

5. Air Travel

Domestic Flights: Airlines like Aeromexico and Volaris offer affordable flights for longer distances, such as Mexico City to Cancun or Los Cabos.

6. Walking

Many cities, especially historical centers, are very pedestrian-friendly and are best explored on foot.

 **Monetary Advice**

Currency is the Mexican Peso (MXN); the exchange rate in October 2024 being approximately 19.4 pesos to a U.S. dollar, or 21.3 pesos to a euro.

Although credit cards and US dollars are widely accepted in most large cities and tourist destinations, you may need Mexican pesos for transactions in rural areas, local markets, and with smaller vendors.

Keep in mind that bargaining is a common practice in Mexico, especially in street markets, flea markets, and at beach vendors. However, bargaining is not typically done in shops and stores in Mexico City, or in resort areas and name brand department stores.

Tipping is not mandatory, but it's generally appreciated for good service. Here's a quick summary of tipping norms:

- **RESTAURANTS**: 10-15% for regular dining, 15-20% for higher-end places. Check if the tip is already included.
- **HOTELS**: Bellhops and concierges: 20-50 pesos ($0.99 - $2.46 USD); housekeeping: 20-50 pesos ($0.99 - $2.46 USD) per day.
- **TAXIS/RIDE-SHARING**: Round up the fare or leave 10-15%.
- **TOUR GUIDES**: 50-100 pesos ($2.46 - $4.93 USD) per person for tours.
- **SPAS/SALONS**: 110-15% of the service cost.
- **BARS**: 10-20 pesos ($0.49 - $0.99 USD) per drink or 10% of the bill.

Mexico's Hospitality

Mexican hospitality is renowned for its warmth, generosity, and deep-rooted sense of community. It's more than just offering a place to stay or food—it's about making people feel like part of the family.

The first thing you'll often notice is the genuine warmth and enthusiasm with which people greet you. Whether you're a stranger or a friend, Mexicans will often greet you with a smile and make you feel immediately at home. It's common to be greeted with phrases like *"¡Bienvenidos!"* (Welcome!) or *"¡Qué gusto verte!"* (What a joy to see you!).

Sharing food is a central part of Mexican hospitality. Even if you're just visiting for a short time, the host will often offer you something to eat, even if it's just a small snack. Meals are often seen as an opportunity to connect and refusing them is usually seen as impolite.

Traditional foods like tacos, tamales, or enchiladas might be served, and the host may go out of their way to prepare a special dish for you.

However, hospitality often extends beyond just a meal or a drink. Mexicans are known for their attention to guests' comfort. If you're staying at someone's house, they might make sure you have everything you need.

Mexican hospitality also comes with an underlying sense of respect for the guest. It's customary to show appreciation for the host's kindness, often through gestures like a thank-you note or a small gift when leaving. Showing respect to the host's culture and traditions always goes a long way!

CUSTOMS

CUSTOMS

Travelers Entering Mexico

 **To enter Mexico, you'll need to meet the following requirements:**

- **Valid passport :** Your passport must be valid for at least six months after your departure date and have at least one blank page.
- **Tourist card[2]:** Also known as the Forma Migratoria Multiple (FMM), you can apply for this card online or at the airport. The card grants you the right to visit Mexico for up to 180 days. However, some airports may require a printed copy of the card. *
- **Customs declaration form:** You'll need to fill out a customs declaration form.
- **Vehicle permit:** If you're driving into Mexico, you'll need a valid Temporary Vehicle Importation Permit and the sticker for it on your windshield. You'll also need your driver's license and documentation showing your migratory status.

---

2   As of September 2024, the Mexico Tourist Card is no longer required for flying into certain Mexican airports.

- **Additional documents:** Mexican immigration officers may request additional documents depending on the purpose of your trip.

For a travel advisory prior to your travels, please consult the US Department of State[3], or your country's Embassy.

 ## When landing in Mexico, you can expect to:

- **Pass through immigration:** You'll need to present your passport and any required visa. You may also need to provide a completed customs declaration form and proof of return.
- **Go through customs:** You'll need to declare any goods you're bringing into Mexico. You'll receive a customs form to fill out during your flight. At the customs checkpoint, you'll hand the form to a customs agent and press a button that looks like a traffic light. A green light means you can go, and a red light means your bags will be inspected.
- **Collect your luggage:** You'll be directed to the baggage claim area to pick up your bags.
- **Find transportation:** You can find car rental agencies, tour operators, shuttles, private ground transportation, and taxis near the airport exit.

Customs Entitlements and Monetary Restrictions

Mexican immigration and customs authorities have strict guidelines on which items can and cannot be brought into the country. This includes restricted quantities of some duty-free items and currency.

---

3   https://travel.state.gov

In general, travelers are allowed to bring goods with a value of up to US$500 into Mexico when traveling by air. If you arrive at a land border, you're allowed to bring up to US$300 worth of goods. It's advisable to carry sales receipts or invoices showing the value of any technological goods or valuable items.

Even though you can bring items such as tobacco and vaping products, alcohol, and medicines into Mexico, there are restrictions on the quantity you can bring with you.

You're allowed to bring medication for personal use, but you will need to declare any medication you're carrying as you go through customs. If you're bringing prescription drugs with you, you'll need a signed letter from your doctor, specifying the type and quantity of medication, the required daily dose, and your doctor's name, contact info and professional license number. Alternatively, you can bring a copy of your prescription, but it must be translated into Spanish.

If you're unsure about Mexico's customs policies, you should check the rules before you travel to avoid problems on arrival.

Money and Monetary Instruments

Mexico allows visitors to bring amounts under $10,000 USD (or the equivalent in other currencies) without needing to declare it. You must notify customs officials upon arrival if you're carrying $10,000 or more. Failure to do this may result in fines or confiscation of funds above the limit. Keeping a record of the source of your funds and the reason for bringing them into the country can help avoid complications.

 Complying with Mexico's customs regulations is essential for a smooth arrival and to prevent legal issues that could negatively impact your trip.

Restricted and Prohibited Items

The following items are prohibited or restricted:

- Narcotics
- Arms and ammunitions
- Live fish
- Predators of any size
- Images representing children in a degrading or ridiculing way
- Used clothes that are not part of personal luggage
- Firearms and ammunitions
- Electronic cigarettes (as of February 2020)

A complete list of these items and their HS codes can be found on the *Prohibited Items List* at the Mexican Customs Rules website.

 **Five Practical Tips to Know Before You Go**

1. Restroom doors marked with an "M" are for the ladies, "H" or" C" for gentlemen.
2. Toilet paper goes in the trash bin; do NOT flush!
3. Build in extra time for everything.
4. Mexico's bus network is actually top notch, but buying bus or plane tickets online can be tricky.
5. Beware of car rental scams and expect to pay local car insurance.

CRIME IN MEXICO

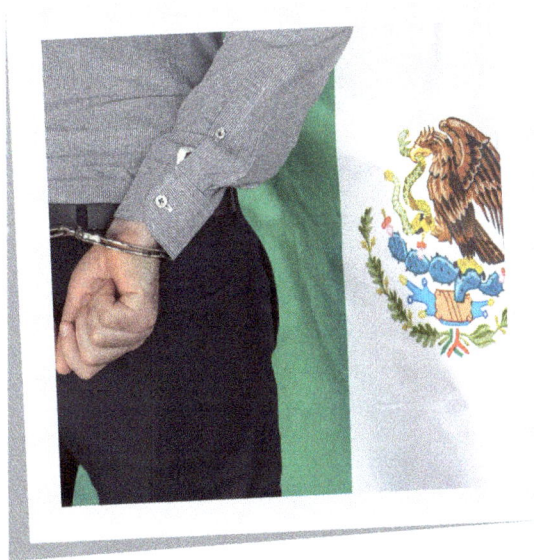

- Overview
- Crime Statistics
- Quick Safety Tips

CRIME IN MEXICO

Overview

While the beauty of Mexico is undeniable and its charm hard to resist, a traveler must be vigilant. Mexico is a vast and diverse country, and while the large majority of tourists experience Mexico safely, it's crucial to be aware of the potential risks and take necessary precautions. Generally, most tourist destinations, including Cancun, Playa del Carmen, Tulum, Puerto Vallarta, and Los Cabos, have a strong presence of tourism police and generally experience lower crime rates. Nevertheless, even in these areas, it's wise to stay alert, especially at night.

Certain regions in Mexico experience higher crime rates, particularly those bordering the United States. The U.S. State Department advises travelers to exercise extreme caution in these areas, and to reconsider travel to some specific states altogether as the U.S. government has limited ability to provide emergency services to U.S. citizens in many areas of Mexico. In many states, local emergency services are limited outside the state capital or major cities. Please refer to the individual states' advisories at the U.S Department of State before traveling.[4]

---

4   https://travel.state.gov/content/travel/en/traveladvisories/traveladvisories/mexico-travel-advisory.html

Mexico is a popular travel destination known for its vibrant culture, beautiful landscapes, and historic cities. While many areas are safe for tourists, crime does exist, and it's important to be aware of the situation to ensure a safe visit.

Crime Statistics

Mexico has a bad rap when it comes to crime. It is a country that often makes international headlines due to widespread violence, drug trafficking, kidnappings, human rights violations and organized crime. According to the *Global Initiative Against Transnational Organized Crime*, Mexico is the fourth most crime-ridden country in the world and the second most dangerous in the Americas!

While this is indeed a scary statistic, it shouldn't outright deter you from visiting Mexico. First, understand that most of these crimes are related to drug trafficking and as such, concentrated to areas where cartels conduct their business. As the chart below illustrates, the surge in violent crime over the past eight years is attributable almost entirely to increased conflict between organized crime groups. For example, last year an estimated 60% of all murders were related to Mexican drug cartels infighting; also note the declining trend in the violent crime level since its height in 2019.[5]

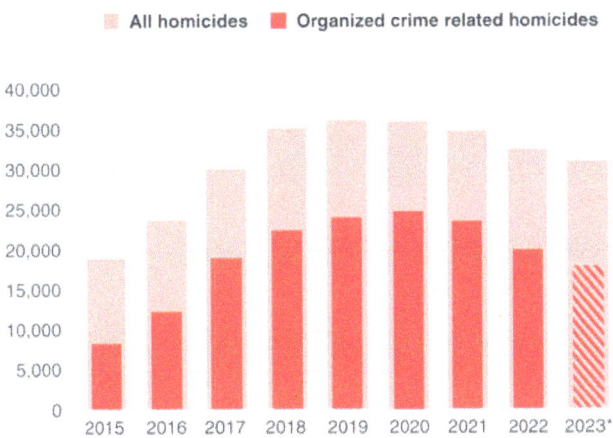

Source: SESNSP, Lantia Intelligence, IEP calculations

As a general rule, the most violent areas are in those Mexican states where no single cartel has total domination as crime groups compete for control. While it is true that Mexico faces challenges related to organized crime, it's important to understand that most of the violence is concentrated in specific areas and is often linked to criminal activities such as drug trafficking and human trafficking. This violence is often targeted at locals involved in the drug trade, and tourists are rarely the target. In fact, the most commonly reported transgression reported by visitors to Mexico is related to petty crimes such as pickpocketing and purse snatchings in crowded areas like markets, public transportation, and tourist hotspots. Scams targeting tourists, such as overcharging for services, fake taxi scams, or unofficial tour guides, are also frequent. Travelers should use reputable services, agree on prices in advance, and stay alert to avoid being scammed.

---

5   https://livewellmexico.com/post/how-dangerous-is-mexico-really

While crime does exist in certain areas of Mexico, millions of tourists visit the country each year without encountering serious issues. By staying aware of your surroundings, choosing safe areas, and following basic precautions, you can enjoy a safe and memorable trip.

 ## Quick Safety Tips

- **Be aware of your surroundings:** Be aware of what's happening around you and keep your belongings close.

- **Avoid certain areas:** Avoid protests, large public gatherings, and areas where illicit activities occur. In popular spring break destinations, exercise extra caution in downtown areas, especially after dark.

- **Be careful with your belongings:** Don't draw attention to your money or business affairs. Keep a photocopy of your passport and other important documents separate from the originals. Store valuables in a safe place.

- **Be careful with alcohol:** Be mindful of your alcohol intake and be aware of counterfeit alcohol.

- **Stay connected:** Keep your phone charged and share your travel plans with friends or family.

- **Know who to call:** Make a list of emergency phone numbers and keep them handy.

- **Check the travel advisory:** Check your government's travel advisory for the most up-to-date information.

- **Bring extra cash:** It's not unusual for a doctor or hospital to demand payment in cash for emergency medical attention.

CHAPTER 4
CRIMINAL LAW VIOLATIONS

- Marijuana and Other Drugs in Mexico
- Prescription Medication
- Penalties
- General Questions
- Law of the Land Hypothetical
- Takeaways

CRIMINAL LAW VIOLATIONS

Marijuana and Other Drugs in Mexico

Mexico's relationship with cannabis is a long and complex one. Marijuana has been cultivated in Mexico since the early 16th century, primarily for industrial uses like rope and textiles, while people used it widely for "medicinal" and religious purposes. However, in 1920, recreational cannabis was banned, and in 1927, exports were prohibited. These policies were influenced by the anti-marijuana movement in the U.S. During the 20th century, marijuana became criminalized across the country.

In 2009, possession of small amounts of marijuana was decriminalized, and between 2015 and 2018, the Mexican Supreme Court made rulings that loosened restrictions on recreational cannabis, determining that the prohibition of medical marijuana infringed on the constitutional right to health. In June 2021, the Court further ruled that the prohibition of personal cannabis use was unconstitutional by a vote of 8-3, legalizing recreational marijuana use for adults and possession of up to 28 grams.[6]

Under the new law, anyone over the age of 18 in Mexico is allowed to purchase and possess less than 28 grams of cannabis. However, possessing higher amounts can result in legal consequences, including monetary fines and a prison sentence. Cultivation of more than eight plants is

---

6   https://weedmaps.com/learn/laws-and-regulations/
     mexico#legislation-history

equally prohibited, as is smoking cannabis in public, especially in front of children.[7]

As a result of the 2009 drug law reforms, the Mexican government adopted legislation decriminalizing possession of small amounts of drugs for "personal and immediate use": up to half a gram of cocaine, five grams of marijuana, 50 milligrams of heroin, 40 milligrams of methamphetamine and 0.015 milligrams of LSD. Again, bear in mind that these quantities are extremely low and that the same rules do not apply to Mexican citizens and visitors. A person can be considered a "small-scale trafficker" even where there is no indication that the quantities they possess are for sale.[8]

Prescription Medication

If you need to take prescription drugs while in Mexico, make sure you have all the necessary paperwork (a doctor's letter or prescription), translated into Spanish. Just be aware that some medications that are legal in your home country may not be considered as such in Mexico, and you can be in legal trouble for possessing a controlled substance. Over-the-counter medicines that contain stimulants, such as codeine and pseudoephedrine, a common ingredient in Actifed, Sudafed and Vicks inhalers, are also prohibited.[9]

Penalties

As a traveler, be aware that the recent changes in law only apply to Mexican citizens, and the rules for **international visitors** remain

---

7   https://www.brookings.edu/articles/mexicos-cannabis-legalization-and-comparisons-with-colombia-lebanon-and-canada/

8   https://www.forbes.com/sites/laurabegleybloom/2019/11/08/is-it-safe-to-travel-to-mexico/#41aea88d2e22

9   safety/north-america/mexico/laws-and-legal-issues-you-need-to-know-about-before-going-to-mexico

unclear. According to the *Mexico News Daily*, "tourists could face stricter consequences" if caught with marijuana.

The United States Embassy and Consulates on Mexico's official site, warn that drug possession and use, including medical marijuana, is illegal in Mexico and may result in a lengthy jail sentence. Furthermore, traveling internationally with medical marijuana is highly discouraged due to the complex and varying drug laws in different countries. Many countries have strict penalties for cannabis possession, and even possessing a medical marijuana card from your home country may not provide legal protection abroad. Mexican officials may not be sympathetic to your glaucoma, anxiety, or other medical condition and will not recognize your medical marijuana card! If you are found bringing marijuana or unauthorized medication in any form into Mexico, you will go to jail. Penalties imposed for drug offenses in Mexico are strict! If you are convicted of such a crime, you could face large fines and jail sentences of up to 25 years.

General Questions

1. *Is cannabis legal in Mexico?* **Yes and no.** Cannabis is still somewhat of a gray area in Mexico. Although use of medicinal and recreational marijuana for adults and possession of up to 28 grams has been legalized in 2021, not all jurisdictions in Mexico recognize this law. Although there are numerous reports that local police are known to turn a blind eye with some tourists when it comes to cannabis and cannabis derivatives (aided by a few dollars under the table), it would be foolish to rely on such a practice as a matter of rule.

2. *Where can I legally purchase marijuana in Mexico?* The legality of purchasing marijuana in Mexico is also a gray area. Since it can easily be grown outside in Mexico, people do grow it, and it can be procured on the street in a number of tourist-friendly towns and cities.

Some larger cities now host a growing gray market of dispensaries, cafes, spas, massage studios, and even restaurants where you can purchase and smoke THC products. Due to the ambiguous legality, these businesses don't advertise in tourist magazines, but rather thrive on word of mouth.[10]

3. *Can I have marijuana on my person or in a hotel room in Mexico?* Strictly speaking, as a non-citizen, possession and consumption of marijuana in public is considered **illegal**. "Drug possession and use, including medical marijuana, is illegal in Mexico and may result in a lengthy jail sentence," the statement from the United States Embassy and Consulates in Mexico warns. Depending on the moral character of the police you encounter, they can and will search you and impose penalties.

4. *Are there any other exceptions to the possession and consumption of cannabis in Mexico?* In short, **no**. Remember, while the law allows personal use for citizens, tourists may face stricter rules. Many international visitors may not be familiar with the limits, and consuming cannabis in public or exceeding the personal possession limit can result in fines or arrest.

---

10 https://www.leafly.com/news/
lifestyle/a-visitors-guide-to-not-quite-legal-weed-in-mexico

5. *What are the penalties for possessing and consuming other types of illicit drugs in Mexico?* Penalties for using illicit drugs can range from **fines and community service** for small amounts of personal use, to significant **jail time** for possession or trafficking larger quantities, depending on the specific drug and the circumstances of the case. However, Mexico does not currently have a policy of criminalizing personal drug use and focuses more on rehabilitation programs for users caught with small amounts, which is not the case if caught with larger amounts of drugs. Monetary fines and prison sentences are severe, and you do not want to find yourself entangled in the Mexican legal system.

 **Law of the Land Hypothetical**

HYPOTHETICAL: *Karen and Jessica are vacationing in beautiful Mexico City. After a spectacular dinner at one of the many outstanding restaurants, the ladies decide to party it up at the dive bar down the street from their hotel. After a night of partying, the girls are exhausted and a friendly local offers to sell them a little pick me up. "Why not? While on vacation..." they think and hand over the money.*

Walking to the hotel in the wee hours of the morning, the girls are stopped by the police. Since they smell of alcohol and weed, the police search them. They find a small pouch containing a white substance, and weighing the content, it turns out the girls are in possession of 502 mg of cocaine. Are Karen and Jessica in trouble?

ANSWER: *It depends. Strictly speaking,* **yes***: they are carrying 502 mg of cocaine with the legal limit being 500mg. No matter how small the difference, any amount of cocaine that exceeds the legal limit can lead to imprisonment and fines. Also, as non-citizens, any quantity of drugs, no matter how small, is considered illegal and can have dire consequences for our two fun-seeking visitors. However, the ultimate outcome depends on the intervening police officer and if they are prepared to turn a blind eye to the situation.*

Takeaways

- While it is legal to possess up to 28g of marijuana, and small quantities of opium, cocaine, heroin, LSD and methamphetamines, these laws apply only to Mexican citizens.

- For visitors, drug possession and use of any drug, including cannabis, is illegal and can result in high monetary fines and even imprisonment.

- If you use prescription medication and you need to bring it with you when you are traveling in Mexico, make sure you have your doctor's note and/or prescription, translated into Spanish.

ALCOHOL-RELATED OFFENSES

ALCOHOL-RELATED OFFENSES

Alcohol-Related Offenses

Alcohol is ingrained into Mexican history and culture. The indigenous people of Mexico cultivated agave to produce pulque, a fermented beverage, long before the Spanish arrived and introduced distillation techniques to create tequila, which today is widely recognized as a key symbol of Mexican culture and identity.

Alcohol is often integrated into celebrations, social gatherings, and traditional practices; with a long history of producing and consuming these beverages, particularly in the form of "fiesta drinking" where large quantities are consumed on special occasions. The typical Mexican drinks include tequila, margarita, mezcal, and Mexican beer.

While alcohol is legal and widely available, alcohol consumption is regulated by both federal and state laws, with the primary legal framework governing the sale, distribution, and consumption of alcohol established in the *General Health Law* and local regulations.

 **Things to Remember**

- **Drinking Age:** The legal drinking age in Mexico is 18. Selling or providing alcohol to individuals under this age is prohibited. Violations of this law can result in fines for businesses and potential criminal charges for individuals involved in supplying minors with alcohol.

- **ID:** You might be required to present an acceptable form of ID, such as a driver's license or passport, to purchase alcohol. (Yes, they do card you in Mexico too!).

- **Public consumption:** It is illegal to drink alcohol in the street or carry open containers in public.

- **Public drunkenness:** In Mexico, the punishment for being drunk in public can include a fine, jail time, or both, as public intoxication is considered illegal and enforced at the municipal level, meaning the specific penalties may vary depending on the location in public spaces. Disorderly conduct, especially involving violence or disturbing the peace, can also lead to criminal charges.

- **Drunk Driving:** Driving under the influence of alcohol is a serious offense in Mexico. In most Mexican states, the limit for blood-alcohol level is 0.8, but in states like Veracruz, Jalisco, and Chihuahua, that threshold is even less. Mexican authorities employ DUI checkpoints to enforce the law and rental cars with tourists are often pulled over. You can end up spending 36 hours in jail, face fines up to $2,500, and can even be denied future entry into the country. In some cases, if an individual is involved in a traffic accident while intoxicated, they may face harsher penalties, including criminal charges for reckless driving or vehicular manslaughter. So be smart, don't drink and drive even when on vacation in the land of tequila!

- **Purchase of alcohol:** Most Mexican states allow stores, restaurants, and bars to sell alcohol 24 hours a day. However, there are some state specific restrictions. For example, in Cancun, packaged alcohol cannot be purchased after 11 PM, and in many border cities, liquor cannot be purchased after 3 PM on Sunday and until 7

AM on Monday. These restrictions are aimed at curbing excessive drinking and associated problems.

- **Alcohol Permits:** If you are hosting an event that will serve alcohol in a public space, you should check if a permit is required.

- **Illegal Alcohol:** The sale of counterfeit or illegal alcohol is a serious crime in Mexico. Illegally produced or unlicensed alcohol, often associated with bootlegging, poses significant health risks and is subject to severe penalties. These include heavy fines and imprisonment, particularly when the illegal alcohol causes harm or death.[11]

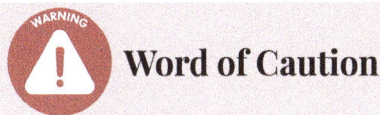

Word of Caution

Lately several instances of poisoning due to tainted alcohol have been reported in different parts of Mexico. Tainted alcohol can contain methanol, a poison that can cause nausea, chest pain, hyperventilation, blindness, and coma. A toxic amount is only about 10 to 30 milliliters, which is approximately the amount of a shot.[12]

To prevent that kind of scenario, choose bottled or canned drinks or drinks from a bottle you watch being opened. Don't leave your drinks unattended! Stick to alcohol brands that you know and if you think your drink tastes or looks off, don't drink it!

If you start feeling sick, seek medical attention right away. Report the incident with the Mexican Federal Commission for the Protection against Sanitary Risk (COFEPRIS) online, by calling +52 01-8—033-5050, or by visiting a COFEPRIS office. If you're a U.S. citizen, contact the U.S. Embassy Consular office for help.[13]

---

11 https://www.mexperience.com/mexico-essentials/practical-information/

12 https://www.usatoday.com/story/travel/news/2017/07/28/
expert-tips-avoiding-tainted-alcohol-mexico/518368001/

13 https://mx.usembassy.gov/message-for-u-s-citizens-spring-break-travel

General Questions

1. *Can I drink and drive in Mexico?* **No.** It is illegal to drive in Mexico with a blood alcohol level exceeding the legal limit of .08%. It is important to note that this limit can be even lower in some states. If a police officer in Mexico suspects you may be under the influence, they have the right to pull you over and administer a breathalyzer test.[14]

2. *Can I possess an open container in public?* **No.** It is illegal to possess an open container and consume alcohol in the public streets and sidewalks in Mexico. However, it is legal to have an open container and consume alcohol in designated public areas such as restaurants, bars, or your hotel or resort.

Law of the Land Hypothetical

HYPOTHETICAL: *Jason, a 23-year-old college student visiting Tulum, has been drinking at a beach bar with friends. After a few too many tequila shots, he starts to feel dizzy and unsteady. When leaving the bar, he begins arguing loudly with his friends and causing a scene in the street. A nearby police officer notices his disruptive behavior and approaches. The officer asks Jason to calm down, but he continues to shout and berate the officer. How much trouble is Jason in and what should he do?*

ANSWER: *Jason could be in serious trouble, but the severity of the consequences will depend on how the situation is handled.*

Jason would likely be arrested for public disorder due to his disruptive behavior. In Mexico, public drunkenness and causing a scene in a public area can result in a fine or detention. He would most likely

---

14 https://www.mexpro.com/blog/rules-of-drinking-alcohol-mexico

spend hours or even a night in jail until he sobers up or until his case is processed. An even bigger problem is that he "resisted authority" by arguing and shouting at the police, which can lead to more serious penalties, including more time in jail and a higher fine.

The best course of action would be for Jason to calm down and be respectful to avoid further escalation and reduce the severity of the outcome. He could:

- Pay the fine if it's offered, which is often the quickest resolution in cases of public intoxication.

- Request to be taken to a sobering center instead of jail if available. In some places, there are facilities where people are allowed to sober up under police supervision without facing criminal charges.

- Have his friends help. If they're able to pay the fine or secure his release, he can avoid jail and get home without too much hassle.

 **Takeaways**

- **Don't drink and drive in Mexico:** Foreigners do not get any leniency for driving drunk. If you hurt or kill someone in the process, you will end up in serious trouble and face the prospect of a long prison sentence in a Mexican jail. Your country's consulate will not be able to shield you from prosecution!

- If you drink, take a cab. Taxis are very affordable in Mexico and there is absolutely no need to drive a car if you are drinking!

- Many places in the interior of Mexico are situated at altitude (for example, Mexico City, Guadalajara and most colonial cities); at high altitudes, alcohol will have more effect on you than if you were drinking at, or close to sea level.[15]

---

15   https://www.mexperience.com/mexico-essentials/practical-information/

- Drink responsibly and don't draw attention to yourself with loud and disruptive behavior. The police could be right around the corner, and they generally don't tolerate displays of public disorder.

- Stop drinking if you start to feel sick and seek medical attention.

FIREARM & AMMUNITION OFFENSES

FIREARM & AMMUNITION OFFENSES

Current Firearm Status

According to a report by the *Small Arms Survey*, it is estimated that there are around 16 million firearms in Mexico. However, only about 2.5 million of these are legally registered. The rest, more than 13 million, are believed to be illegal and are often smuggled from the United States, contributing significantly to violence from organized crime and drug cartels.[16]

In 2021, 32% of all homicides in Mexico were committed using firearms, according to data from the National Institute of Statistics and Geography (INEGI). This percentage has remained consistently high due to the proliferation of illegal weapons, particularly in regions affected by organized crime.[17]

Not surprisingly, Mexico has strict firearm laws, which are governed primarily by the Federal Law of Firearms and Explosives. Here's a brief overview of the current firearm status:

---

16   https://www.smallarmssurvey.org/

17   https://www.inegi.org.mx/

1. General Firearm Ownership

- Private ownership of firearms is highly restricted. Only individuals with a special permit from the Mexican government can legally own a firearm.
- Citizens can only legally possess firearms for self-defense, hunting, or sport shooting, and they must apply for a license.
- Most civilians are limited to owning small-caliber firearms (caliber .22 and similar) and must follow strict regulations.
- Automatic and military-grade weapons are banned for civilian ownership.

2. The Role of the Military and Law Enforcement

- In Mexico, firearms are largely controlled by the military. The Mexican Army oversees the issuance of firearm licenses and the importation of weapons.
- Only the Army and select government agencies can possess and use high-caliber or military-grade weapons.

3. License and Background Checks

- To own a firearm legally, individuals must pass a rigorous background check and meet specific requirements, including psychological evaluations and proficiency tests.
- The applicant must also demonstrate a valid reason for firearm ownership, such as self-defense, hunting, or sport shooting.
- A firearm license must be renewed every three years.

4. Restrictions on Firearm Locations

- Firearms are prohibited in public spaces and can only be carried in specific cases, typically for self-defense or professional reasons (e.g., security personnel).

- Firearms must be registered and carrying or transporting a firearm outside of a designated area (like a shooting range) or without the necessary paperwork is illegal.

5. Gun Stores and Imports

- There is only one legal gun store in Mexico, located in Mexico City, under the control of the military. This store sells mostly small-caliber guns, ammunition, and related accessories. The purchase process involves background checks and strict oversight.
- Importing firearms without proper authorization is illegal. The vast majority of firearms in Mexico are believed to enter the country illegally, often smuggled across the border from the U.S.

6. Impact of Drug Cartels and Violence

- Despite strict laws, illegal firearms are widely available in Mexico, and organized crime—especially drug cartels—has access to high-powered weaponry. This has led to a growing issue of gun violence, which remains a serious problem in many regions of the country.
- The illegal arms trade between the U.S. and Mexico is a major issue, with many firearms smuggled into Mexico to supply criminal groups.

 **Penalties**[18]

In Mexico, firearm violations and crimes are met with severe legal consequences, reflecting the country's strict gun control policies. The penalties for these offenses vary depending on the nature of the violation,

---

18   https://tile.loc.gov/storage-services/service/ll/llgl-rd/2019669439/2019669439.pdf

the type of weapon involved, and whether the firearm was used in the commission of a crime:

- **Possession of Illegal Firearms:** One of the most serious offenses in Mexico is the illegal possession of firearms. Anyone found with a firearm without the proper permit, or with restricted or military-grade weapons, can face heavy penalties. Generally, those caught in possession of unauthorized firearms can be sentenced to **5 to 15 years** in prison. The severity of the penalty increases significantly if the individual is found in possession of high-caliber or automatic weapons, with prison sentences ranging from **10 to 20 years** in such cases.

- **Trafficking and Smuggling Firearms:** Illegal arms trafficking, or smuggling firearms into Mexico, is another grave offense. Those caught trafficking firearms face **5 to 15 years** in prison, depending on the scale and scope of the trafficking operation. If the firearms involved are high-powered, military-grade, or linked to criminal organizations, sentences can rise to **10 to 20 years.**

- **Firearm Use in Crimes:** The use of firearms in the commission of a crime is treated as an aggravating factor under Mexican law. Whether the firearm is used in a robbery, kidnapping, or assault, the penalties are severe. For example, if a firearm is used during a robbery, the individual may face **5 to 15 years** in prison. However, if a firearm is used in more serious violent crimes, like homicide, the penalties increase to **25 to 50 years**, depending on whether the crime was intentional, premeditated, or aggravated in nature.

- **Unauthorized Carrying of Firearms:** Even carrying a firearm without proper authorization—whether or not the weapon is registered—carries significant penalties. Individuals caught carrying a firearm in public without a license or in prohibited areas, such as government buildings or airports, can be sentenced to **5 to 10 years** in prison, depending on the circumstances.

- **Penalties for Organized Crime Involvement:** For individuals involved in organized crime, the penalties are even harsher. If firearms are linked to cartel activities or other forms of organized crime, the punishment can be as severe as **20 to 40 years** in prison.

The Mexican government treats firearms possession in the context of organized crime as a serious national security threat, given the role of cartels in perpetuating violence across the country.

- **Special Circumstances and Military-Grade Weapons:** In Mexico, the penalties are even more severe when it comes to military-grade weapons. The possession of assault rifles, machine guns, or grenade launchers without authorization carries one of the harshest penalties—between **15 to 30 years** in prison. This is due to the potential for these weapons to cause mass harm, particularly when in the hands of organized crime groups.

- **Juvenile Offenses:** If a minor is caught with a firearm without proper authorization, the penalties are different but still serious. In such cases, minors may be placed in juvenile detention facilities or may face rehabilitation programs designed to deter further criminal behavior. The approach is more rehabilitative, aiming to correct the path of younger offenders.

? General Questions

1. *What happens if the police catch me carrying a firearm in Mexico?* If the police catch you carrying a firearm in Mexico without the proper permit, you can face serious consequences, including 5 to 10 years in prison for carrying an unregistered firearm. The firearm will be confiscated, and you may also face fines. Even if you're a foreign tourist, ignorance of the law is not a valid defense.

2. *What is the potential sentence for a firearms violation upon conviction?* The potential sentence for a firearms violation in Mexico, such as possessing an unregistered firearm, is typically 5 to 15 years in prison. The sentence can increase to 10 to 20 years if the firearm is high-powered or associated with organized crime.

 **Law of the Land Hypothetical**

HYPOTHETICAL: *Jessica, a 34-year-old tourist from the United States, is visiting Mexico for a vacation in Playa del Carmen. She owns a legally registered handgun back home and has a concealed carry permit. While in Mexico, Jessica plans to explore some remote areas and, feeling concerned about safety, she decides to bring her firearm with her. She carefully packs it in her luggage, believing that since she owns the gun legally, it won't be a problem. However, during a routine luggage check at Cancún International Airport, security officers discover the gun. Jessica is immediately arrested for possession of an unregistered firearm in Mexico. What legal consequences could Jessica face under Mexican law for bringing her unregistered firearm into the country?*

ANSWER: *Mexico's Federal Law of Firearms and Explosives strictly prohibits tourists from bringing firearms into the country without proper permits. Even though Jessica is unaware that bringing a firearm into Mexico is illegal, ignorance of the law is not a defense. Jessica could face 5 to 15 years in prison, with her firearm being confiscated. The fact that she is a tourist may not result in leniency, though diplomatic efforts or legal counsel might help mitigate her sentence.*

Law of the Land True Story

Jason J. Johnson, a 35-year-old American tourist was searched during a routine traffic stop in Tijuana, Mexico, in 2019. Officers discovered a small-caliber pistol in the glove compartment, along with a few rounds of ammunition. Johnson had been visiting Tijuana for the day, crossing the border for some sightseeing. Johnson, who had a valid U.S. concealed carry permit, was unaware that it was highly illegal to bring a firearm across the Mexican border without specific authorization. Johnson was promptly arrested for illegal possession of a firearm. He was detained for several days before being brought before a judge. Although Johnson's legal team tried to argue that he had no malicious intent and was simply unaware of the law, the Mexican legal system does not offer leniency for such violations.

Ultimately, Johnson was sentenced to 8 months in prison and had to pay a substantial fine. He was later released early for good behavior, but the case raised significant attention, especially for those who regularly cross into Mexico from the U.S. This example demonstrates how easy it can be for tourists to run afoul of Mexico's strict gun laws, even when they have legal ownership of their firearm in their home country.

Takeaways

- **Strict Laws:** Mexico has very strict firearm regulations; unauthorized possession is illegal.

- **Severe Penalties:** Violations can lead to 5 to 15 years in prison even for less egregious violations.

- **No Exceptions for Tourists:** Foreigners are treated the same as locals.

- **Ignorance Is Not a Defense:** Not knowing the law doesn't prevent arrest or prosecution.

- **Firearm Confiscation:** Illegal firearms will be seized.
- **High Risk at Borders:** Bringing firearms across the border without a permit is highly risky.

PROSTITUTION

IN THIS CHAPTER

- Overview
- Law and Penalties
- Prostitution Practices
- Sex Trafficking and Exploitation
- Sex Tourism and Public Health
- Tips to Avoid Being Solicited
- Law of the Land Hypothetical
- Current Situation

PROSTITUTION

Overview

Prostitution in Mexico is a multifaceted issue that spans legal, social, and economic dimensions. While sex work is decriminalized and regulated in certain zones, many sex workers remain vulnerable to exploitation, trafficking, and unsafe working conditions. Economic inequality, migration, and the prevalence of organized crime all contribute to the complexity of the issue. There is a growing recognition of the need for better legal protections for sex workers, a stronger emphasis on public health, and continued efforts to combat human trafficking, and there are efforts made to improve the status and safety of sex workers in Mexico. The challenge is not just about the regulation of prostitution itself but also about improving the conditions that drive people into sex work in the first place.

 **Laws and Penalties**

Prostitution in Mexico is legal under the federal law, but it is regulated at the local level. This means each state and municipality can have its own rules and regulations governing the practice, including the operation of brothels, escort services, and street prostitution. Penalties for prostitution can include arrest, fines, and community service.

In many Mexican cities, prostitution is allowed in designated areas, commonly referred to as "tolerance zones." These zones are typically located in specific areas, such as certain districts in larger cities (e.g., Mexico City, Tijuana, and Guadalajara). In these zones, sex work is tolerated and often regulated through health checks, licensing, and other requirements to ensure the safety and health of sex workers and their clients. Sex workers are also required to undergo regular health check-ups, including testing for STDs. Local authorities may also require sex workers to carry identification cards or permits, which help monitor the profession and ensure that it complies with the local regulations.

Brothels are legal in some areas but are heavily regulated. In places where they are permitted, they usually need to adhere to strict operational guidelines and must comply with local health regulations. Independent sex workers, or those working as escorts, can also operate legally, provided they comply with any local licensing requirements.

Street prostitution is more controversial and often subject to stricter local ordinances. In many cities, street prostitution is either regulated or criminalized in certain areas, leading to frequent police sweeps and arrests in places where sex work is not permitted.[19] [20]

Prostitution Practices

The estimated number of prostitutes in Mexico as of 2019 is around 240,000.[21] Although street-based prostitution is the most visible form and receives the most attention, it represents only a small proportion of the sex industry, which also includes brothels, escort services, and online prostitution.

Brothels (often referred to as "casas de citas" or "casas de masajes") can be found in various forms, ranging from high-end establishments to

---

19   https://revista.drclas.harvard.edu/
     sex-work-law-and-police-in-mexico-city

20   https://en.wikipedia.org/wiki/Prostitution_in_Mexico

21   https://en.wikipedia.org/wiki/Prostitution_statistics_by_country

more informal or lower-end venues. Some brothels are fully legal and regulated, often requiring licenses and operating under a legal framework that ensures health checks for sex workers and protection from exploitation. Again, the level of regulation varies widely across the country, and many brothels operate illegally, either through bribes or by flying under the radar of local authorities.

Many sex workers in Mexico operate as escorts, offering services through online platforms, social media, or specialized websites. This form of sex work is often marketed as more private, discrete, and often targets higher-paying clients. The rise of apps and websites has made it easier for sex workers to advertise and find clients, but this also sometimes leads to increased risks, such as exploitation, violence, or lack of legal protection.

Sex Trafficking and Exploitation

While prostitution itself is largely legal in Mexico, human trafficking, exploitation, and child prostitution are illegal and punishable by law. Mexico has been making efforts to combat sex trafficking, with strict laws against coercion and the involvement of minors in prostitution; however, organized crime, corruption, and economic instability contribute to the persistence of this problem.

While the Mexican government has taken steps to combat human trafficking, the effectiveness of these efforts is debated, as the problem persists due to insufficient resources, corruption, and the sheer scale of the issue. International organizations, non-governmental organizations (NGOs), and human rights groups, have been working to raise awareness of these issues, advocating for better protection of sex workers, stronger law enforcement against traffickers, and comprehensive social programs to address the root causes of exploitation.

Victims, particularly women and girls from impoverished or marginalized communities, are often targeted because they are vulnerable. Economic hardship, lack of education, and a desire for better opportunities make them susceptible. Traffickers may promise a better life or job opportunities, especially in larger cities or abroad. Some victims are recruited under the pretense of employment in hospitality, modeling, or other legitimate jobs, only to be forced into sexual exploitation upon arrival.

Once trafficked, victims are often subjected to psychological manipulation and threats to keep them from escaping. This can include threats of violence against them or their families. Traffickers frequently use debt bondage, where the victim is told they must work off an arbitrary or inflated debt, keeping them trapped in exploitation. Victims are often forced to work in brothels, massage parlors, or bars, where they are made to perform sexual services against their will. Some victims are moved across various locations, making it harder for law enforcement to track them. In some cases, traffickers may force victims to engage in online sexual exploitation, including pornography or webcam sex work. Some sex trafficking victims are moved across international borders, including into the United States, to be exploited in the sex trade. This can involve the use of false documents, or in some cases, victims are physically smuggled.

Mexican drug cartels and other organized crime groups are often involved in sex trafficking, using it as a lucrative form of revenue alongside other illegal activities such as drug trafficking and extortion. Corruption among local law enforcement and government officials can make it difficult for victims to seek help. In some cases, traffickers may bribe police officers or other authorities to avoid arrest or punishment.

https://www.amnestyusa.org/countries/mexico/
https://www.hrw.org/world-report/2017/country-chapters/mexico

 ## Sex Tourism and Public Health

Cities like Tijuana, Cancún, and Playa del Carmen are major tourist destinations and often have significant prostitution industries catering to both local clients and tourists. In places like Tijuana, sex work can be highly visible around certain areas near the border with the United States, often catering to foreign men seeking services. In tourist-heavy areas, sex work can be more organized, with advertising, websites, and specialized agencies offering various options for tourists.

The sex industry in Mexico is closely linked to the spread of sexually transmitted diseases due to the nature of high-risk sexual behaviors, including unprotected sex, multiple partners, and lack of consistent access to healthcare. Unfortunately, specific, detailed statistics on STDs among sex workers in Mexico are scarce due to underreporting, stigma, and challenges in data collection.

Studies suggest that about 10-15% of female sex workers in Mexico are living with HIV. This percentage can vary significantly depending on the region and the level of access to healthcare services. Likewise, sex workers, especially those in urban areas or high-tourist zones, are at elevated risk for syphilis. The prevalence of syphilis among sex workers has been reported as high as 10-20% in some studies. The rates of other STDs (Chlamydia, Gonorrhea, Herpes) among sex workers are also notably higher than the general population, with some reports indicating 30-40% of sex workers having at least one of these infections.[22] [23]

---

22 https://www.who.int/data

23 https://www.gob.mx/censida

Tips to Avoid Being Solicited

When traveling in Mexico, especially in popular tourist areas, you may encounter sex workers trying to engage you in conversation or offer services. While it's important to be respectful and polite, there are also strategies to help you to avoid being hassled. Here are some practical tips to avoid unwanted attention from sex workers:

- **Be aware of your surroundings but avoid eye contact**: if you're in areas known for sex work, like certain nightlife districts, you may be approached more frequently. Sex workers may approach you more often if they think you're showing interest, even unintentionally. Avoid making prolonged eye contact, as this can be interpreted as interest.

- **Polite but firm responses:** say "No, gracias" (No, thank you). This is a clear, polite, but firm way to decline an offer.

- **Don't engage in conversation:** If you don't want to be hassled, avoid getting into any conversation or discussion. Simply and politely saying "no" or continuing to walk away is usually effective.

- **Avoid flashing money or valuables:** If you carry visible cash, expensive jewelry, or other valuables, you might attract more attention.

- **Travel in pairs or groups and avoid secluded or dark places:** Sex workers may target tourists in less trafficked, dimly lit areas. Stick to well-lit, populated streets.

- **Report persistent harassment:** If you're being persistently harassed by anyone, including sex workers, and it feels uncomfortable or threatening, you can contact the local police or authorities.

- **Research your destinations:** Before heading out, use apps or maps to familiarize yourself with the safest routes and areas where you're less likely to encounter aggressive solicitation.

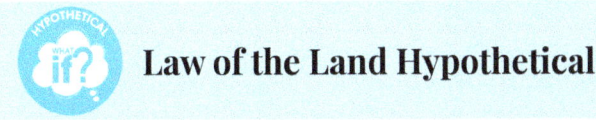

Law of the Land Hypothetical

HYPOTHETICAL: *You're walking through a busy tourist area in Cancún when an attractive woman in her late 20s approaches you. She starts chatting, asking if you're enjoying your vacation and mentions a few nearby clubs. As the conversation continues, it becomes clear she's offering more than just casual company. She says: "I know a place where you can have some real fun, if you're interested." What should you do?*

ANSWER: *Politely decline and stay firm. Smile and say, "No, gracias. I'm just enjoying my night." Keep walking and avoid engaging in any further conversation. If she persists, simply repeat your answer and don't get involved in any back-and-forth. If you feel uncomfortable, remove yourself from the situation as quickly as possible and move to a more crowded or safer area.*

Current Situation

The current situation with prostitution in Mexico is complex, with both regulated and informal sex work occurring across the country. While some areas have legal frameworks that aim to protect sex workers, in many regions, they face significant risks, including violence, exploitation, human trafficking, and health risks due to limited access to medical care and condoms. Efforts are being made to improve conditions for sex workers, but challenges remain, including social stigma, legal gaps, and police harassment.

Prostitution is a significant part of the informal economy in many areas, particularly in tourist-heavy locations. It provides income for many women, but often at the cost of personal safety, health, and social marginalization. Sex work can also be part of larger poverty cycles, especially for women from marginalized communities. Lack of education, job opportunities, and economic inequality drive many into the profession, often under economic coercion.

For travelers, it's important to be aware of the local dynamics, especially in tourist areas, and to take precautions to stay safe while being respectful of the local communities.

LGBTQ

CHAPTER 8

LGBTQ

Homophobia in Mexico

Homophobia in Mexico is a complex issue that varies across regions, communities, and social contexts. In general, attitudes toward LGBTQ+ individuals can range from acceptance to outright hostility, and the level of homophobia often depends on factors such as geography, education, socioeconomic status, and religious beliefs.

A statistic reveals that in 2007 Mexico had the second-highest rate of homophobic crimes in the world after Brazil.[24] Even though it remains a strong Catholic country where traditional notions of "machismo" and gender roles are deeply embedded in the culture, Mexico is becoming increasingly accepting of same-sex relationships and has laws in place to protect those who identify differently.[25]

There are vast regional differences between urban and rural areas. In cities like Mexico City, Guadalajara, and Monterrey, there tends to be more openness and visibility for LGBTQ+ people. Mexico City is often regarded as the LGBTQ+ hub of the country. The city has a large and visible LGBTQ+ community, with Zona Rosa (Pink Zone) being the epicenter of LGBTQ+ life, known for its LGBTQ+-friendly bars, clubs, restaurants, and shops. Mexico City is also home to a massive Pride Parade (Marcha del Orgullo) every June, which draws hundreds of thousands of people,

24 www.intrepidtravel.com/us/mexico/is-mexico-lgbtqia-friendly

25 https://pmc.ncbi.nlm.nih.gov/articles/

making it one of the largest Pride events in Latin America. Mexico City was also one of the first regions in Latin America to legalize same-sex marriage in 2010. Additionally, there are laws that protect against discrimination based on sexual orientation and gender identity in several states. There has been growing visibility for LGBTQ+ rights, with advocacy groups pushing for more protections and education, gaining more acceptance in the media and entertainment sectors.

But while legal protections exist, enforcement can be inconsistent. Some regions may not fully implement these laws, and LGBTQ+ individuals may still face harassment or violence without sufficient legal recourse. Primarily in more rural or conservative regions that have more traditional attitudes, influenced by the strong presence of Catholicism and other conservative religious values, homophobia may be more pronounced, with LGBTQ+ individuals facing greater challenges in terms of social acceptance, family rejection, and discrimination. Hate crimes, including violent attacks, against LGBTQ+ people are a serious concern. Transgender individuals, in particular, are vulnerable to targeted violence, and reports of homophobic attacks, though difficult to track accurately, still occur frequently. In addition, many LGBTQ+ individuals still experience discrimination in the workplace, in educational settings, and within families.[26]

Penalties for Homosexual Activity in Mexico

In Mexico, homosexual activity is not criminalized. In fact, homosexual activity has been legal in Mexico since the late 19th century. The Mexican Penal Code no longer includes laws that criminalize same-sex relations, meaning that consensual sexual activity between consenting adults, regardless of gender, is allowed without legal penalty.

Same-sex marriage is legal in Mexico City and in several other states, including Oaxaca, Querétaro, Baja California, and others. However, it's not universally recognized across the entire country. While some states

---

26 https://pmc.ncbi.nlm.nih.gov/articles/

have legalized same-sex marriage, others still have laws that do not recognize such unions, leading to a patchwork of legal recognition across Mexico.

LGBTQ Tourism and Safety Concerns

Mexico has become a popular and welcoming destination for LGBTQ+ tourism, especially in major cities and coastal areas. Mexico City, Puerto Vallarta, and the Riviera Maya (including Cancún and Playa del Carmen) are key LGBTQ+-friendly destinations. These places offer vibrant LGBTQ+ scenes with bars, clubs, and events, including large Pride parades and festivals.

In Mexico City, the Zona Rosa is a hub for LGBTQ+ life, and the city hosts one of the largest Pride events in Latin America. Puerto Vallarta is known for its inclusive vibe, LGBTQ+-owned businesses, and beach resorts, while Cancún and Playa del Carmen attract LGBTQ+ tourists with their luxury resorts and beach parties.

While LGBTQ+ rights have advanced, legal protections can vary by region, and some rural areas still hold more conservative attitudes. Public displays of affection may be frowned upon outside major tourist zones. Overall, Mexico offers a welcoming environment in its tourist hotspots, with a growing emphasis on LGBTQ+ inclusivity.

General Questions

1. *Do laws in Mexico protect homosexual expressions and conduct?* **Yes**, Mexico protects homosexual expressions and conduct. Same-sex marriage is legal in several states, including Mexico City, and there are anti-discrimination laws in place in many areas that protect LGBTQ+ individuals in employment, housing, and public services. However, the level of protection can vary by region.

2. *What is the punishment for homosexual expressions and conduct?* In Mexico, there are no punishments for homosexual expressions or conduct. Same-sex relations between consenting adults are legal, and LGBTQ+ individuals are not subject to criminal penalties for their sexual orientation or behavior. However, in rural and more conservative areas displays of affection may be frowned upon and are discouraged.

Law of the Land True Story

In June 2024, the Mexican Supreme Court issued a groundbreaking decision ordering the state of Guanajuato to recognize the gender identity of transgender individuals on official documents, marking a significant advancement for transgender rights in Mexico.[27]

The ruling stemmed from a legal challenge filed by a transgender woman who sought to have her gender identity legally recognized in Guanajuato, a state that had previously denied her request. Despite the existence of gender recognition laws in other parts of Mexico, such as Mexico City and a few other states, Guanajuato did not have such

---

27 https://www.hrw.org/news/2024/06/10/
    court-orders-guanajuato-mexico-recognize-trans-identities

legal provisions in place. The case highlighted the disparity in legal protections and recognition for transgender individuals across different regions of Mexico, especially in more conservative areas.

The plaintiff argued that the state's refusal to update her gender marker on her official identification documents—such as her birth certificate—was a violation of her right to equality and self-determination, which are protected under Mexico's Constitution and human rights law. The Supreme Court of Mexico ruled in favor of the transgender woman, stating that gender self-identification is a fundamental human right under the Mexican Constitution. The court emphasized that gender identity should be respected, and transgender individuals have the right to modify their gender markers on official documents without requiring surgery or any medical intervention.

The court also ruled that it was discriminatory to deny transgender people the right to self-determine their gender. This decision reinforced the principle of equality and upheld the rights of transgender individuals to live free from discrimination and to have their identity legally recognized. The ruling effectively mandated the state of Guanajuato to allow transgender individuals to change their gender marker on official documents, aligning it with the legal standards established in other parts of Mexico. The ruling is seen as a victory for gender equality and transgender rights activists, as it expands the scope of gender recognition to regions where such protections have previously been lacking. By enforcing this change, the court also sends a powerful message that transgender rights are human rights, and governments must respect and protect those rights uniformly across the country.

 **Law of the Land Hypothetical**

HYPOTHETICAL: *Louis and Gabriel, a same-sex couple in Monterrey, Mexico, face exclusion and mistreatment at work after revealing their relationship. Luis is passed over for a promotion, and Gabriel is given less favorable tasks. They suspect their treatment is due to their sexual*

orientation. They file a discrimination complaint with the Mexican Federal Labor Board and seek support from an LGBTQ+ rights group.

ANSWER: *The Mexican Federal Labor Board investigates and finds the company guilty of violating the Mexican Federal Labor Law and the Constitution. The couple is awarded compensation for lost wages, and the company must adopt anti-discrimination policies.*

SEXUALLY MOTIVATED/ VIOLENT CRIMES

SEXUALLY MOTIVATED/ VIOLENT CRIMES

Overview

Sexually motivated crimes are a significant and growing issue in Mexico, impacting countless individuals, mostly women and children. Sexually motivated crimes are acts of sexual violence or exploitation driven by a desire to dominate, control, or harm the victim. In Mexico, these crimes include a range of offenses of varying degrees:

- **Sexual harassment (Acoso sexual):** Unwanted advances, comments, or gestures, often occurring in public spaces, workplaces, or educational institutions.

- **Sexual assault (Abuso sexual):** Non-consensual physical contact or forced sexual acts.

- **Rape (Violación):** Non-consensual sexual penetration, typically involving threats, coercion, or violence.

- **Human trafficking and exploitation (Trata de personas):** The forced exploitation of individuals—especially women and children—for sexual services.

The statistics surrounding sexually motivated crimes in Mexico are har-rowing. According to official reports and studies, the situation is dire:

- One in five women in Mexico has experienced some form of sexual violence in her lifetime, with a significant number of these cases involving rape or sexual assault.

- A 2018 survey found that 47% of women in Mexico reported having been victims of sexual harassment, including in public spaces, workplaces, and educational institutions.

- Mexico has one of the highest femicide (the intentional killing of women and girls because of their gender) rates in the world. In 2022 alone, there were 968 reported cases of femicides, a 127 percent increase from 2015. At present, about one in four female killings in Mexico are classified as femicides.

According to the Interior Ministry's most recent data (2019), only 2 percent of women who were victims of violence received help. Of all cases of domestic violence, only 5 percent were prosecuted and only 1 percent resulted in convictions.[28]

Despite these alarming figures, underreporting remains a major issue. Many victims feel shame, fear retribution, or believe that authorities will not take their cases seriously. This underreporting means that the true scale of the problem is even larger than the numbers suggest.

Such sexually motivated crimes in Mexico are fueled by a combination of social, cultural, and economic factors. In many parts of Mexican society, patriarchal attitudes and machismo (a strong sense of male dominance) persist, normalizing the objectification and subjugation of women. Women are often seen as inferior, leading to an environment where sexual violence can be minimized or tolerated. Furthermore, in some regions, organized crime and drug cartels are deeply involved in sex trafficking, exploiting vulnerable women and children for profit. This adds another layer of complexity to the issue, as the power and reach of these

---

28 https://www.state.gov/reports/2022-coun-
     try-reports-on-human-rights-practices/
     mexico

criminal organizations often intimidate or overpower local authorities. At the same time, increasing access to the internet perpetuates online sexual exploitation—such as revenge porn, cyberstalking, and the trafficking of explicit images.

In recent years, Mexico has passed several legal reforms to strengthen its response to sexual violence. The Ley Olimpia, passed in 2020, criminalizes revenge porn and other forms of digital sexual violence, giving victims legal recourse in the fight against cyber exploitation. In 2022, Mexico's Supreme Court ruled that consent should be the central element in cases of sexual violence, expanding the legal definition of rape to prioritize the presence of explicit consent.[29]

Federal law criminalizes the rape of men and women, including spousal rape, and conviction carries penalties of up to 20 years of imprisonment.

Federal law also prohibits domestic violence and stipulates penalties for conviction of between six months and four years of imprisonment.[30]

---

29 www.visionofhumanity.org/gender-based-violence-in-mexico/

30 https://www.state.gov/reports/2022-coun-try-reports-on-human-rights-practices/mexico

General Questions

1. *Do laws in Mexico related to sex crimes protect the victims equally?* While laws exist to protect victims, the systemic failures within the legal and enforcement mechanisms often lead to unequal treatment, with the most vulnerable victims facing the greatest barriers to justice.

   For example, gender bias within the justice system often leads to cases being dismissed or victims being blamed for the violence they experience, especially in cases of sexual assault. Victims, especially those from vulnerable or marginalized communities, often face re-victimization during legal proceedings, which discourages them from coming forward. Femicides, or gender-based killings of women, are still common, and many cases go unpunished due to the lack of investigation or accountability.

2. *Pursuant to law, what is the age of consent for sex in Mexico?* In Mexico, the age of consent for sexual activity is **17 years old**. This means that individuals under the age of 17 are legally unable to give consent to sexual activity, and any sexual relations with someone under this age are considered statutory rape, even if there is no force or coercion involved.

   However, the law does contain some exceptions, such as the "close-in-age" rule (known as *"La Ley de Consentimiento Sexual"*), which allows minors who are close in age (typically within 3 years of age) to engage in sexual activity without it being considered a crime. This exception is designed to prevent the criminalization of consensual sexual relationships among teenagers but still protects younger minors from sexual exploitation.

Law of the Land Hypothetical

HYPOTHETICAL: *Maria, a 24-year-old woman, works as a cashier in a busy shopping mall in Mexico City. Over the past few weeks, she has noticed a man regularly coming into the store, making lewd comments and making her feel uncomfortable. Despite her attempts to ignore him, he continues to make advances and even follows her out of the store after her shift. One evening, as she walks to her car in the parking lot, the man approaches her, grabs her arm, and tries to forcefully kiss her. Maria screams and pushes him away, but he manages to escape before anyone arrives. She is shaken and immediately calls the police, reporting the incident. What legal protections does Maria have in this situation?*

ANSWER: *Maria has legal protections under Mexico's General Law on Women's Access to a Life Free from Violence, which covers sexual harassment, assault, and other forms of gender-based violence. Maria can file a formal complaint of sexual harassment or sexual assault, depending on the severity of the encounter.*

Takeaways

- Sexual violence, including harassment, assault, and femicide, is widespread in Mexico, with millions of women and children affected each year. The country has one of the highest femicide rates in the world, signaling a serious crisis of gender-based violence.

- Legal protections for victims exist, but corruption, impunity, and gender bias within law enforcement and the judiciary often prevent justice from being served, leading to underreporting and continued trauma for survivors.

- Deep-rooted issues like machismo, gender inequality, and victim-blaming perpetuate sexual violence in Mexico, normalizing abusive behaviors and allowing perpetrators to escape accountability.

- Real change requires educating future generations about consent and gender equality, alongside a shift in societal attitudes toward women. Comprehensive action, including stronger legal enforcement and greater victim support, is essential to tackling this issue.

ARRESTED IN MEXICO

CHAPTER 10
ARRESTED IN MEXICO

Overview

When traveling in a foreign country, it's imperative to recognize that you are subject to the legal jurisdiction and regulations of that particular nation. These laws may significantly differ from those in your home country and might not offer the same legal protections you are accustomed to. It's crucial to bear in mind that penalties for violating foreign laws can be more severe than those for similar offenses in your home country, and ignorance of these laws is not typically accepted as a defense.

The consequences for breaking the law while abroad can be severe and may include expulsion, fines, arrest, or imprisonment. Even unintentional violations can lead to serious legal repercussions. It is essential for travelers to be aware of and adhere to the laws of the host country to avoid legal entanglements and ensure a safe and enjoyable experience.

Specifically, stringent penalties are often enforced for possession, use, or trafficking of illegal drugs in many countries. Convicted offenders can expect severe consequences, including lengthy jail sentences and hefty fines. The legal processes for foreigners in the event of an arrest abroad involve being charged or indicted, prosecuted, potentially convicted and sentenced, and, if applicable, going through an appeals process.

Navigating a foreign legal system can be complex, and individuals arrested abroad must be prepared to comply with the legal procedures of the host country. Seeking legal representation and understanding the local legal nuances are crucial steps for those facing legal issues in a foreign jurisdiction.

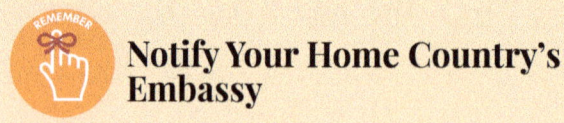

Notify Your Home Country's Embassy

If you or a family member are arrested, local authorities must notify your country's embassy under the Vienna Convention. You may ask that local police contact your embassy on your behalf.

Arrest Process

According to the *Federal Code on Criminal Proceedings*, serious crimes are those that have a negative effect on the fundamental values of Mexican society. Therefore, any foreigner coming into Mexico must abide by the laws or risk being arrested on criminal charges.

Most common criminal charges result from:[31]

- **Drug Offenses:** Possessing, using, or trafficking drugs in Mexico can lead to severe penalties, including imprisonment.
- **Alcohol and Drugs:** Being under the influence of drugs or alcohol in public places can result in fines or arrest.
- **Public Disorder:** Acts such as disturbing the peace, engaging in public fights, or causing a disturbance can result in fines or jail time.

---

31 https://www.meneseslegal.com/english/
what-kind-of-criminal-charges-can-foreigners-end-up-with-in-mexico/

- **Traffic Violations:** Serious infractions, like driving under the influence or causing an accident, can also carry legal penalties. The article below stresses the importance of understanding Mexican laws and the local legal system to avoid complications. It recommends foreigners consult with a legal professional if they are in any legal trouble in Mexico.

- **Immigration Violations:** Staying beyond the allowed time on a tourist visa or working without proper permits can lead to deportation or fines.

- **Assault:** Even minor altercations or physical confrontations can result in legal trouble.

- **Sexual Offenses:** These charges are treated very seriously and may include sexual harassment, assault, or abuse.

- **Theft and Property Crimes:** Theft, fraud, or property damage can lead to significant legal consequences.

 Upon arrest, the person must pass through Mexico's foreign legal system, which includes charge or indictment, prosecution, conviction, and sentencing. After the sentencing hearing, a person has the right to appeal the verdict. They also have the right to a public or private legal counsel to represent them during the court proceedings. Also bear in mind that Mexico and the US share criminal records through the International Criminal Police Organization (INTERPOL). So even if a person is only prosecuted in Mexico, their records will be available in the US and may lead to problems during background checks for jobs or loans. What happens in Mexico doesn't always stay in Mexico![32]

- **Arrest:** In Mexico, the arrest process follows a legal procedure designed to protect the rights of the accused, although it can vary depending on the situation (such as whether the arrest is made with or without a warrant). In

---

32 https://www2.texasattorneygeneral.gov/files/cj/article4.pdf

an arrest with a warrant, a judge issues an arrest warrant based on probable cause, often after reviewing evidence presented by the police or public prosecutor (Ministerio Público). Arrest without a warrant, on the other hand, happens if a police officer witnesses a crime being committed (flagrancia, or in flagrante delicto), or if the person is found with significant evidence linking them to a crime.

- **Preliminary Investigation:** Once arrested, the person is taken into custody and the authorities (police or the public prosecutor) begin a preliminary investigation. This phase can last several days. The public prosecutor may gather evidence, question witnesses, and hold interviews to establish whether there is sufficient evidence to pursue charges.

- **Initial Hearing (Audiencia Inicial):** The prosecutor presents the evidence or reason for the arrest to the judge. The defense attorney can challenge the arrest and evidence, argue for bail, or request other conditions. Within 48 hours, the judge must decide whether the person will remain in detention, be released on bail, or be released with other conditions (like house arrest).

- **Formal Charges:** If the judge finds sufficient grounds, formal charges are brought, and the legal process continues. If the person is not charged, they must be released immediately. However, if the case proceeds, a trial phase will begin.

- **Pre-Trial Detention:** If the person is deemed a flight risk or there's a danger of them interfering with the investigation, they may be held in pre-trial detention (prisión preventiva) until the trial. This can last for several months, depending on the case.

- **Trial:** In Mexico, the justice system operates on a "trial by oral" model, where all evidence and arguments are presented openly in front of a judge. Both the prosecutor and defense attorney present their cases. The accused person has the right to attend the trial, challenge evidence, and cross-examine witnesses. A verdict is issued, and depending on the outcome, the person may be acquitted or convicted.

- **Appeal:** If convicted, the defendant has the right to appeal the sentence. The appeal is reviewed by a higher court, which can either confirm the verdict or modify the punishment.

 ## Juveniles

If the person arrested is under 18, the process differs slightly, and special courts handle cases involving minors. Juvenile arrests in Mexico are governed by the National Law for the Criminal Justice System for Adolescents Age of Criminal Responsibility in Mexico is generally 12 years. Children under this age cannot be held criminally responsible for their actions.

When juveniles are arrested, they are typically placed in specialized detention centers designed for minors. These facilities aim to provide educational and rehabilitative services rather than solely punitive measures. In many cases, alternatives to detention, such as community service or probation, may be pursued, especially for first-time or minor offenders.

 ## Immigration Cases

- If someone is arrested for immigration-related offenses, they may face deportation proceedings in addition to criminal prosecution.

- It's important to remember that while these steps are meant to follow legal procedure, in practice, there can be delays, and sometimes human rights concerns have been raised, particularly in cases of pre-trial detention or abuses during arrest.

Rights of the Arrested Person

If you find yourself in a legal predicament, it is crucial to understand your rights to ensure that you are treated fairly and to protect your legal interests. Under Mexican law, you have the following protections: [33]

- **Right to remain silent:** You cannot be compelled to self-incriminate.
- **Right to legal counsel:** You must be informed of your right to have an attorney present, and if you can't afford one, the state will provide a public defender (Defensor Público).
- **Right to be informed of the charges:** You must be told the reasons for your arrest.
- **Right to a prompt hearing:** Within 48 hours of arrest, you must be presented before a judge, who will decide whether to formally charge you and whether you should remain in detention or be released.

Getting Legal Assistance

Under Mexican law, anyone who is arrested has the right to legal counsel. If you cannot afford a lawyer, the court will assign a public defender to aid your legal representation.

Upon arrest, law enforcement is required to inform you of your rights, including your right to have a lawyer present during questioning. You have the right to choose your own lawyer and it's advisable to contact one as soon as possible after your arrest.

If you are a foreign national, you should notify your embassy or consulate immediately. American citizens may also wish to notify the U.S.

---

33 https://mx.usembassy.gov/arrest-of-a-u-s-citizen/

Embassy or consulate of the arrest using the *American Citizens Services Contact Form*.[34] They can help contact family, friends, or employers of the detained U.S. citizen with their written consent, visit the detained U.S. citizen in jail, help ensure that prison officials provide appropriate medical care, explain the local criminal justice and legal processes, and most importantly, connect you to local attorneys who speak English.[35] Bear in mind, their powers are limited and they cannot get U.S. citizens out of jail, provide legal advice or represent U.S. citizens in court, serve as official interpreters or translators, nor can they pay your legal, medical, or other fees.[36]

 If you find yourself in need of an English-speaking attorney while in Mexico, please visit the following site: **https://mx.usembassy.gov/arrest-of-a-u-s-citizen/**

 ## State Department Website

If you encounter any of the following scenarios

- Lost/stolen passports abroad
- What the Department of State Can and Can't Do in a Crisis
- Help for U.S. Citizen Victims of Crime, U.S. Citizens Missing Abroad
- Ways to Locate your Loved One in a Crisis Abroad
- Arrest or Detention of a U.S. Citizen Abroad
- Crimes Against Minors Abroad, Emergency Financial Assistance for U.S. Citizens Abroad

---

34 https://mx.usembassy.gov/contact/

35 https://mx.usembassy.gov/local-resources/

36 https://mx.usembassy.gov/arrest-of-a-u-s-citizen/#

- Protecting Yourself from Scams
- International Maritime Piracy and Armed Robbery at Sea
- Forced Marriage
- Terrorism
- Information for U.S. Citizens about a U.S. Government-Assisted Evacuation
- Crisis and Disasters Abroad

Consult the following website:
https://travel.state.gov/content/travel/en/international-travel/ emergencies/arrest-detention

Bail

Although Mexico has a bail system, it works differently than in some other countries. It is governed by the Federal Criminal Procedure Code, but the specifics can vary by state and the nature of the charges. Here are some key points about how bail works In Mexico:

1. Bail is typically available for non-violent offenses. In cases of serious crimes, particularly those related to organized crime, bail may be denied outright.

2. Judges have significant discretion in determining whether to grant bail. They consider factors such as the severity of the offense, flight risk, and the defendant's criminal history.

3. If bail is granted, the judge will set a specific amount. Defendants or their families can pay this amount directly or through a bail bond agency.

4. In cases where bail is not granted, defendants may be held in "preventive detention" while awaiting trial. This can be for an extended period, depending on the complexity of the case.

5. If released on bail, defendants may have to adhere to certain conditions, such as regular check-ins with authorities, restrictions on travel, and wearing monitoring devices.

6. Defendants can appeal a decision to deny bail, but the process can be lengthy and complex.

There are several options for bail bondsmen in Mexico. Simply google "bail bonds" in the city where you are traveling.

Complaints Against Police

In Mexico, the relationship between the police and the community is fraught with tension and distrust. Many citizens share stories of encounters that highlight deep-rooted issues within law enforcement. Corruption is a recurring theme; people recount experiences of officers demanding bribes in exchange for basic services, like the return of stolen property or the promise of safe passage. This pervasive corruption not only erodes public trust but also creates an environment where crime can flourish.

Many people believe that officers face little to no consequences for their actions. Additionally, the police force often struggles with inefficiency and inadequate resources and their police responses to emergencies are frequently slow and disorganized. With insufficient training and equipment, officers find it challenging to effectively investigate crimes and ensure public safety.

Human rights violations further complicate the picture. Numerous accounts emerge of excessive use of force, unlawful detentions, and even torture. Victims often feel powerless, knowing that the very institutions meant to protect them can turn against them. Therefore, exposing such offenses is crucial although effectively complaining about police misconduct in Mexico can be challenging.

To file a complaint against the police in Mexico, you can go to a local police station and file a *denuncia* (police report) or contact the *Ministerio Público* (equivalent to a district attorney) in the jurisdiction where the incident occurred; you can also call emergency services at 911 to report the issue. If you are a U.S. citizen, consider contacting the U.S. Embassy in Mexico for assistance in navigating the complaint process. You are also always encouraged to contact human rights organizations and expose any violations. To get results, you have to be determined and persistent!

Here is contact information for most visible human rights organizations in Mexico:

Contact information for Human Rights Organizations

The Office of the United Nations High Commissioner for Human Rights (OHCHR)

Phone: +41 22 917 92 48
E-mail: oacnudh@ohchr.org.
Address: Alejandro Dumas 165, Colonia Polanco, Delegación Miguel Hidalgo, CP 11560, México, D.F.

Amnesty International

Address: Calle Luz Saviñon 519 Colonia del Valle, Benito Juarez 03100 Ciudad de Mexico.

The International Committee of the Red Cross (ICRC)

WhatsApp: +521 55 80 12 90 55.
Website: irc.org/en/document/mexico-working-mexican-red-cross

Mexican Commission for the Defense and Promotion of Human Rights((CMPDPH)

E-mail: contact@idpc.net

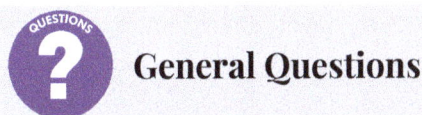

General Questions

1. ***If I am convicted in Mexico, am I likely to be released on bail pending the outcome of my appeal?*** Whether you can be released on bail pending the outcome of an appeal depends on several factors, including the nature of the crime and the specifics of your case. Bail may be more likely for non-violent offenses. For serious crimes, especially those related to organized crime or violence, bail is often denied. The decision to grant bail pending an appeal is ultimately at the discretion of the judge.

2. ***What influences a bail determination?*** The severity of the crime is a primary factor. Non-violent and less serious offenses are more likely to receive bail, while serious crimes, especially those involving violence or organized crime, may result in bail being denied.

   Judges also assess whether the defendant poses a flight risk. Factors like the defendant's ties to the community, family connections, and travel history can influence this assessment. A defendant's prior criminal record can affect bail decisions. A history of reoffending or previous failures to appear in court can lead to stricter bail conditions or denial.

   The strength of the evidence against the defendant may play a role. If the evidence is compelling, a judge might be less inclined to grant bail. The defendant's behavior during the arrest and initial court appearances can influence the judge's decision. A respectful and compliant demeanor may positively impact the outcome.

   Effective advocacy by a lawyer can significantly impact the outcome. A skilled attorney can present a compelling case for bail and address concerns raised by the prosecution.

3. *Who is entitled to bail?* The right to bail is generally provided only for individuals accused of non-serious crimes, first time offenders, and those who do not pose the risk of flight.

4. *If I am arrested, how soon will I see a judge or magistrate?* If you're arrested in Mexico, you should see a judge within 48 hours. This is in accordance with Mexican law, which requires that individuals be brought before a judge promptly to determine the legality of the detention and decide on measures such as bail or pretrial detention. If this time frame is not met, the individual may be released.

5. *Will I be able to contact my country's embassy in Mexico?* If you are arrested in Mexico, you have the right to contact your embassy or consulate. It's advisable to inform the authorities of your nationality so they can facilitate your access to consular assistance. The embassy can provide legal support and help communicate with family or friends.

CHAPTER 11

JAILS VS. PRISONS: CONDITIONS & CULTURE

JAILS VS. PRISONS: CONDITIONS & CULTURE

Overview

As is the case everywhere, similarly in Mexico the primary purpose of jails and prisons within the criminal justice system is to detain individuals convicted of crimes, serving to punish offenders, deter future criminal activity, incapacitate them from committing further crimes, and in some cases, rehabilitate them to reintegrate into society. The Mexican imprisonment system is a complex landscape marked by significant challenges and deep-rooted issues.

There are some key differences between jails and prisons to be aware of. Jails, known as *centros de detención*, serve primarily to hold individuals awaiting trial or those serving short sentences, typically less than a year, for minor crimes. They are typically operated by municipal or state governments. This local control can lead to significant variations in management and conditions between different facilities. In many cases, local police departments are responsible for the administration and oversight of these jails.

In contrast, prisons, or *penitenciarías*, are designed for long-term incarceration of individuals convicted of serious crimes. The prison system in Mexico is classified into various security levels—minimum, medium, and maximum—depending on the nature of the offenses committed.

Federal prisons are operated by the national government, specifically through the *Ministry of Security and Citizen Protection*. These facilities house inmates convicted of federal crimes. State prisons are managed by individual state governments, leading to differences in conditions, resources, and rehabilitation programs across the country.

The conditions in Mexican jails and prisons paint a stark picture of a system grappling with serious challenges. Overcrowding is a pervasive issue, with many facilities operating far beyond their intended capacity. As of 2024, the prison population in Mexico is close to 234,000, with an occupancy level of over 104%![37] Inmates often find themselves crammed into cramped quarters, where personal space is a luxury and basic amenities are in short supply. This overcrowding not only makes daily life uncomfortable but also exacerbates health and safety concerns.

Sanitation is another major issue. Many jails and prisons struggle to maintain adequate hygiene, leading to unsanitary living conditions that can affect the health of inmates. Access to clean water and proper sanitation facilities is often limited, leaving many without the basics needed for personal care. Medical care is similarly lacking, with long waits for treatment and insufficient access to necessary healthcare services, making it difficult for inmates to receive the care they need.

Violence is a major problem in both jails and prisons. Gangs often dominate the environment, exerting control and influence over other inmates. This leads to a culture of intimidation and fear, where conflicts can escalate quickly, putting lives at risk. Corruption among staff further complicates matters, as reports of bribery and favoritism create an environment where safety and fairness are not guaranteed.

While some prisons do offer educational and vocational programs aimed at rehabilitation, access to these resources is inconsistent. Many facilities lack the funding and infrastructure to provide adequate support for inmates, leaving them with few opportunities to prepare for life after incarceration. Instead of focusing on rehabilitation, the system

---

37 https://www.prisonstudies.org/country/mexico

often leans more toward punishment, which can hinder successful reintegration into society.

Human rights issues are prevalent as well, with numerous reports highlighting mistreatment, lack of due process, and inadequate legal representation. In this challenging environment, the experiences of inmates reveal the urgent need for reform and improvement within Mexico's penal system.

Corruption has infiltrated the system, contributing to a culture of fear and insecurity. Inmates frequently encounter threats to their safety, and staff integrity can be compromised by corrupt practices. Reports of human rights violations, such as inadequate healthcare and lack of proper legal representation, paint a troubling picture of the treatment of individuals within these facilities.

 A Mexican jail or prison is not somewhere where you want to find yourself on your trip. But if you do, remain calm, keep a low profile, familiarize yourself with your rights, document everything, and perhaps most importantly, seek legal representation ASAP!

 General Questions

1. ***What is the difference between a jail and prison in Mexico?*** In Mexico, jails and prisons serve distinct roles within the criminal justice system. Jails (*centros de detención*) are primarily for short-term confinement, holding individuals awaiting trial or serving brief sentences for minor offenses. They often experience overcrowding and offer limited rehabilitation opportunities, leading to a chaotic environment with a high turnover of inmates.

In contrast, prisons (*penitenciarías*) are designed for long-term incarceration of those convicted of serious crimes. They typically provide more established systems and may offer rehabilitation programs, although access can vary. Prisons are managed by the federal government or state authorities, leading to differences in security and oversight.

The legal processes also differ; inmates in jails are often in the midst of ongoing legal proceedings, while those in prisons are serving defined sentences.

2. *Do jails and prisons offer religious services to inmates?* **Yes,** jails and prisons in Mexico generally offer religious services to inmates. Many facilities have designated areas for worship and may provide access to religious leaders from various faiths, allowing inmates to participate in services, prayer meetings, and other spiritual activities.

These services can provide emotional support and a sense of community for inmates, contributing to their overall well-being. However, the availability and frequency of these services can vary significantly from one facility to another, often depending on resources and the management of the institution.

3. *How do prisoners spend their time?* In Mexican jails and prisons, inmates spend their time in various ways, depending on the resources and rules of each facility. Many participate in work programs, engaging in tasks like manufacturing or maintenance, which help them earn small wages and develop skills.

Education is another important aspect, with some facilities offering literacy and vocational training, though access can be inconsistent. Recreational activities may include sports or games, but opportunities vary widely.

Religious services provide spiritual support and foster community among inmates. Socializing with fellow inmates is common, as they share meals and experiences, helping build camaraderie.

However, inmates also face periods of isolation or lockdown, especially during security incidents, and spend time addressing their legal matters as they prepare for court dates or meet with lawyers. Overall, daily life in these facilities is a mix of work, education, and the challenges of confinement.

4. *What type of jobs can inmates perform?* It is crucial for inmates to perform some kind of job while incarcerated. These job opportunities not only help them develop skills and earn a small income but also provide a sense of purpose during their time in confinement.

Inmates may work in factories producing goods such as clothing, furniture, or crafts, contributing to the prison economy and gaining vocational skills. Some facilities have agricultural programs where inmates can work on farms, growing crops or raising livestock, which provides food for the prison and practical farming experience. Many inmates work in the kitchen, preparing meals for themselves and others. This includes cooking, cleaning, and food preparation tasks.

Inmates may also help with facility upkeep, performing maintenance tasks like plumbing, electrical work, or general cleaning to keep the environment functional. Some prisons offer textile jobs where inmates can engage in sewing, mending clothes, or creating other fabric-based products.

Depending on the facility, they may also engage in crafting activities, producing items like pottery, jewelry, or artwork, which can be sold or used for personal use, and in certain cases, they may assist with clerical tasks, such as organizing files or helping with paperwork within the facility.

5. *How does the prison commissary system work in Mexico?*
In Mexican prisons, the commissary system allows inmates to purchase items that supplement what the facility provides. They can buy snacks, hygiene products, clothing, and sometimes small electronics, depending on the facility's offerings.

Inmates typically fund their purchases with money sent from family and friends or earnings from prison jobs. Each facility has its own rules about what can be purchased and how often orders can be placed, with security measures in place to prevent contraband. However, each facility has its own rules regarding what can be bought and how often orders can be placed. Security protocols often limit the quantity or types of items available, ensuring that everything remains under control.

6. *What type of medical care do prisoners receive?* In Mexico, prisoners have the right to medical care, but the quality and availability of services can vary widely. While they generally have access to basic health services, such as routine check-ups and emergency care, overcrowding and underfunding often compromise the quality of care. Specialized medical services and mental health support are typically inadequate, and access to necessary medications can be inconsistent, leading inmates to rely on family for additional supplies. Preventive care measures are also lacking, contributing to the spread of diseases within facilities.

7. *What is prison culture in Mexico?* Prison culture in Mexico is significantly shaped by the gangs, which control many aspects of daily life and create hierarchical structures among inmates. Despite the challenges, a sense of solidarity often develops, with inmates forming close bonds and supporting each other.

Survival strategies are essential, as inmates navigate social dynamics and manage relationships with fellow prisoners and guards. Violence is a common reality, driven by gang rivalries and power struggles, leading to an atmosphere of tension. To cope, inmates engage in work programs, religious services, and creative activities like art and writing, which provide purpose and identity. Cultural practices persist within the prison, allowing inmates to celebrate traditions and maintain connections to their lives outside. Overall, this complex culture is characterized by resilience, adaptation, and community.

HELPING A FRIEND OR RELATIVE IMPRISONED IN MEXICO

HELPING A FRIEND OR RELATIVE IMPRISONED IN MEXICO

Overview

If someone is imprisoned in a foreign country, the most crucial step is to immediately contact the nearest embassy or consulate as they can provide vital assistance like contacting family, finding local legal representation, monitoring the detainee's welfare, and ensuring they receive appropriate medical care within the limits of local laws. If you are a U.S. citizen, you can also reach the State Department emergency line at 1-888-407-4747.

Next, you need to collect details about the arrest, including the charges, location of detention, and any contact information for the imprisoned individual. As soon as possible, hire a local lawyer; the embassy can provide a list of English-speaking attorneys in the country to represent the detained person:[38]

Regularly contact the embassy for updates on the case and to relay any concerns you may have. If at all possible, regularly check on the detained person's well-being and ensure they are treated fairly. If needed, also advocate for proper medical treatment.

---

38 https://mx.usembassy.gov/arrest-of-a-u-s-citizen/

 **Important points to remember:** [39]

- **Limitations of embassy assistance:** While the embassy can provide significant support, they cannot guarantee the release of the imprisoned person or intervene directly in the legal proceedings.

- **Respect local laws:** Always adhere to the laws of the country where the person is detained.

- **Consider legal options:** Depending on the situation, exploring options like prisoner transfer treaties might be possible.

Getting Food to an Inmate

Food in Mexican prisons can vary significantly based on the facility and its resources. Generally, meals are simple and may include staples like beans, rice, tortillas, and occasionally meat or vegetables. Some prisons might allow inmates to buy additional food or have family send supplies, which can improve their diet. Most prisoners typically receive three meals a day, but the quality and quantity can be inconsistent. In some cases, the meals may not meet nutritional standards, leading inmates to rely on external sources for better food options.

While you can bring food to an inmate, there are strict guidelines on what items are permitted. All food should be visible in transparent packaging for security checks and you cannot bring utensils that could be used as weapons. You should always contact the specific prison or jail where the individual is detained to get the exact list of allowed food items and procedures for bringing food to prison.

39 https://travel.state.gov/content/travel/en/international-travel/
emergencies/arrest-detention

Restricted Items

As a general rule, the following are restricted items: [40] [41]

- **Fresh produce with potential for fermentation:** Grapes, pineapples, plantains, and some berries are typically not allowed as they can be used to make alcohol.

- **Raw vegetables and fruits:** Most fruits and vegetables must be peeled and chopped before being brought in.

- **Dairy products:** Restrictions may apply to dairy products like fresh milk or cheese.

- **Unpackaged food:** Food must be in clear packaging to allow for inspection.

- **Homemade meals:** Most prisons do not allow bringing in homemade cooked meals.

Sending Money or Packages to an Inmate

Sending money to someone in a Mexican prison can be a bit complex, as procedures vary by facility. Each prison may have specific rules regarding money transfers. Check the official website or contact the prison directly for guidance.

Many prisons require that you use specific services to send money. Common options include:

---

40 https://www.vice.com/en/article/how-to-eat-well-in-a-mexican-prison

41 https://sensorycriminology.com/2024/03/04/the-aftertaste-of-prison/

- **Money transfer services:** Companies like Western Union, MoneyGram, or Wise may have services tailored for prisons.[42] [43]
- **Bank transfers:** Some prisons allow direct deposits into inmate accounts.[44]

Make sure to adhere to the guidelines provided by the prison or the money transfer service, including limits on amounts and any fees that may apply.

Retain any receipts or confirmation numbers until you confirm the inmate has received the funds. It's always a good idea to do thorough research or seek assistance from someone familiar with the process, as it can vary significantly based on the specific prison and individual circumstances!

It is also possible to send packages to someone in a Mexican prison, but as with everything else, it's important to follow specific rules and regulations. Each facility has its own guidelines about what items are allowed, so you'll need to verify the specific regulations for the prison in question. Typically, only individuals on an approved contact list can send packages, so it's essential to ensure you're documented as an approved sender.

Permissible items often include clothing, hygiene products, and sometimes approved food, but there are usually restrictions on what can be sent. There are several items that are generally prohibited. These include weapons and sharp objects, drugs and alcohol, electronics like cell phones and tablets, and valuables such as cash or jewelry. Inappropriate materials, including adult content or hate speech, are also not allowed. Many prisons restrict sending food items, especially homemade ones, due to safety and hygiene concerns. Additionally, some facilities have rules against clothing with specific logos or designs. Bear in mind that packages are generally inspected by prison authorities before reaching

---

42 https://www.westernunion.com/us/en/send-money-to-mexico.html

43 https://www.moneygram.com/mgo/us/en/m/send-money-to-mexico/

44 You'll typically need the inmate's full name, ID number, and the facility's details to complete the transfer.

the inmate, and you may have to include specific documentation, especially for food or other regulated items. For the most accurate information, it's best to contact the prison directly.

Prisoner Outreach

Prisoner outreach in Mexico focuses on supporting inmates and their families through various programs and initiatives. Organizations often work to provide resources like legal aid, education, and mental health services. They aim to improve living conditions within prisons and advocate for inmates' rights.

Some outreach efforts also involve family support, helping loved ones stay connected through communication programs or assistance with sending packages. Additionally, many organizations work on rehabilitation and reintegration programs, helping former inmates adjust to life after prison.

Volunteers and non-government organizations play a crucial role, often visiting prisons to provide emotional support and facilitate workshops or training sessions. These initiatives strive to create a more humane prison environment and promote social reintegration, ultimately addressing the broader issues of justice and reform in the Mexican penal system.

If you want to get involved, here are some organizations that need your help:

Prison Fellowship International

The largest global network of Christian ministries focused on the criminal justice system. It operates in over 120 countries, aiming to restore and heal through programs that transform offenders, reconcile relationships, and restore communities. The organization is supported by more than 60,000 local volunteers and works through multi-denominational national ministries, providing culturally relevant support to prisoners, their families, and victims. You can make a donation at **https://pfi.org/who-we-are/**.

Criminon

A global non-profit dedicated to criminal rehabilitation and reform, established in New Zealand in 1972. Active around the world, including Latin America and especially Mexico, it offers courses to inmates and correctional staff to improve self-respect, relationship skills, and break destructive habits, aiming to help individuals reintegrate as contributing members of society. By partnering with correctional institutions, Criminon addresses the root causes of criminal behavior to reduce recidivism. Its mission focuses on empowering individuals, promoting dignity and life skills, and creating a more productive society through responsible individuals and healthier communities.

You can reach them at 1-888-837-3523, email at info@criminon.org, and visit their website at **https://www.criminon.org/get-involved/**.

La Cana

An organization that empowers women in prison by providing economic tools and support for personal growth through various workshops and programs. They focus on areas like mental health, self-esteem, addiction prevention, and arts education. Their initiatives help improve inmates' social skills and outlook on the future. Additionally, La Cana collaborates with authorities to develop standards for prison labor and human rights, and they run a Former Prisoners Program to support women after release. They sell handmade products created by the women, with proceeds contributing to their rehabilitation and family support. Overall, La Cana aims to connect inmates with the community and promote positive change in their lives. You can learn more at **https://lacana.mx/**.

⚠️ Prison Scams

You need to be aware of scams related to U.S. prisoners in Mexico that target family members and friends. Common red flags include unsolicited communication, such as unexpected calls or messages claiming to be from a prison or lawyer. Scammers often create a sense of urgency, asking for immediate funds for bail or emergencies and may request sensitive personal information, which legitimate organizations would not do.

They often pressure individuals to act quickly, leaving little time for verification. It's important to verify the identity of anyone claiming to represent a prisoner by checking with official prison contacts or legal representatives before taking any further action. Be cautious of unconventional payment methods, like gift cards or money transfers, which are frequently used by scammers. If you suspect a scam, it's essential to report it to law enforcement and always verify information!

Visiting and Phone Calls

Visiting

In Mexican prisons, arranging visits involves several rules. Family and friends must coordinate with the inmate, as the inmate has the final say on visits. Each prison has specific visiting days, times, and strict dress codes, which should be confirmed with prison authorities or the consulate. Generally, prisoners can receive one visit per week from up to twelve people, but only three can have direct contact at a time. Visitors can only see one inmate per visit, unless they are direct family members.

Mexican law permits conjugal visits for prisoners with their spouses or legal partners, which occur in designated areas after health examinations.

Security measures for these visits can be stringent, including possible strip searches.

Inmates can also receive visits from justice system officers, legal representatives, and religious ministers. While inmates have the right to refuse visits from authorities, it is advisable to have an attorney present during such meetings. Visits from attorneys are typically scheduled on specific days and should be private. Additionally, inmates can request visits from their religious ministers, subject to approval and security restrictions.[45]

Phone Calls

In Mexican prisons, inmates cannot have personal cell phones and must use monitored prison phones for calls. These calls are subject to strict limitations, including who they can call, when they can call, and how long the calls can last, primarily to prevent illegal activities like extortion. Inmates typically make collect calls to pre-approved numbers and usually cannot receive incoming calls. Families must set up accounts with the prison's phone service provider to facilitate these calls, and policies regarding phone access can vary by facility, so it's important to check the specific rules for each prison.

Paying a Fine

If you are found liable in a civil or criminal proceeding in Mexico, you may be required to pay a fine as punishment, which means you will have to financially compensate the court or the affected party for the offense committed; this is a common form of penalty in Mexico, particularly for minor offenses, and can be imposed alongside other punishments like jail time depending on the severity of the case.

In Mexico, **there are no jury trials in either civil or criminal cases**, so the judge decides on the penalty based on the presented evidence. The amount of the fine will depend on the nature of the offense and the

---

45 https://www.gov.uk/government/publications/mexico-prisoner-pack/
prisoner-pack-mexico

specific laws of the jurisdiction. If you disagree with the fine imposed, you can appeal the decision through the legal system. If you fail to pay the fine, the Mexican authorities may take actions like seizing assets or restricting your ability to travel.

To pay a fine in Mexico as part of a civil or criminal proceeding, first determine the fine amount and relevant case details through the issuing court or authority. Visit the appropriate court or legal authority to inquire about accepted payment methods, which may include cash, bank transfers, or online options. Obtain specific payment instructions, including any necessary forms or references. After making the payment, ensure you receive a receipt as proof, which is important for your records. If you have any questions or need assistance, consider consulting a lawyer familiar with Mexican law to help navigate the process. It's crucial to act promptly to avoid additional penalties or complications.

Upon Release

Upon your release from a Mexican prison as a national of another country, several important steps will follow. First, your legal status in Mexico will need to be addressed. Depending on your circumstances, you may face deportation or have the option to remain in the country. If deportation is necessary, immigration authorities might initiate proceedings, and you could be held in an immigration detention center until arrangements for your deportation are made.

It's crucial to contact your home country's embassy or consulate for assistance. They can provide guidance, help with travel documents, and support during your transition back home. Some embassies even offer programs to assist citizens with reintegration, which may include support for housing and employment.

If you are being deported, authorities may arrange your travel back to your home country. However, if you choose to stay in Mexico, you will need to secure the necessary documents, such as a visa. It's also essential to understand any legal obligations or restrictions placed on you after your release, such as the requirement to report to local authorities.

THE ADMINISTRATION OF JUSTICE

THE ADMINISTRATION OF JUSTICE

Mexico's Legal System

 Mexico's legal system is rooted in the *Civil Law* tradition, largely influenced by its historical ties to Spain. This tradition is the oldest and most widely adopted legal system globally. Civil law originated in ancient Rome, evolving from the legal traditions of the Roman Republic and Empire. A key early codification was the Corpus Juris Civilis, compiled under Emperor Justinian in the 6th century AD. The revival of Roman law in European universities during the Middle Ages further developed civil law, especially in Italy. The Napoleonic Code, established in France in 1804, was a significant milestone, providing a comprehensive legal framework that influenced many countries. Consequently, civil law became the predominant legal tradition in Europe, Latin America, and beyond.[46]

Civil law, in a legal context, refers to a legal system based on written codes and statutes, as opposed to case law or judicial precedents. Civil law systems are typically codified, meaning laws are organized into

---

46 https://lawlibrary.arizona.edu/mexican-legal-system

comprehensive written codes covering various areas, such as civil, criminal, commercial, and administrative law.

In civil law jurisdictions, statutes and codes are the primary sources of law. Judges interpret and apply these laws but do not create new law through their rulings. Legal proceedings often follow an inquisitorial model, where judges take an active role in investigating the facts of a case, as opposed to the adversarial system found in common law jurisdictions. Civil law primarily governs private rights and obligations, including contracts, property, family law, and torts. Its systematic approach is designed to facilitate the administration of justice and provide a consistent legal framework.

Mexico's legal system consists of several key components:[47]

1. **Constitution:** The Mexican Constitution of 1917 is the supreme law of the land, outlining fundamental rights, the structure of government, and the legal framework.

2. **Legal Codes:** The system is primarily codified, with major codes that govern various areas of law, including:

    -   **Civil Code:** Covers personal rights, contracts, family law, property, and inheritance.

    -   **Criminal Code:** Defines criminal offenses and establishes penalties.

    -   **Commercial Code:** Regulates business transactions and commercial relationships.

3. **Judicial Structure:**

    -   **Supreme Court of Justice:** The highest court, addressing constitutional and federal matters.

    -   **Federal and State Courts:** Handle civil, criminal, and administrative cases at various levels.

---

47 https://law-arizona.libguides.com/

4. **Legal Procedures:** The system generally follows an inquisitorial model, where judges take an active role in investigating cases and gathering evidence.

5. **Rights and Protections:** The legal framework emphasizes individual rights and provides mechanisms for legal protection, including the amparo action to protect constitutional rights.

6. **Administrative Law:** Governs the activities of government agencies and public administration

 **The Judiciary**

The judiciary in Mexico plays a crucial role in upholding the rule of law, protecting individual rights, and ensuring the proper application of justice. Rooted in the country's commitment to constitutional governance, the Mexican judiciary is structured to address both federal and state legal matters, reflecting the complexities of a diverse and populous nation.

At the top of the judiciary is the *Supreme Court of Justice*, which serves as the highest judicial authority in Mexico. Established by the Constitution of 1917, the Court is tasked with interpreting constitutional provisions, resolving disputes between states and the federal government and ensuring the uniform application of federal law. It has the power to review lower court rulings, making its decisions binding on all other courts. The Supreme Court's role is particularly significant in safeguarding constitutional rights, as it adjudicates cases that involve fundamental freedoms and civil liberties.

Beneath the Supreme Court, the *federal court system* handles cases related to federal laws and issues, including specialized courts that address administrative, labor, and electoral matters. This structure ensures that legal disputes involving federal statutes are managed uniformly across the country. Additionally, federal judges are tasked with protecting citizens' rights, particularly in cases where government actions may infringe upon individual freedoms.

At the *state level*, each of Mexico's 32 states maintains its own judiciary, consisting of *trial courts, appellate courts, and a state supreme court*. These state courts handle a wide range of civil, criminal, and administrative cases based on local laws. The decentralized nature of the judiciary allows for responsiveness to regional legal issues and the specific needs of local populations.[48]

Mexico also has several special courts designed to address specific areas of law and types of cases. These include:

1. **Administrative Courts:** These courts handle disputes involving administrative law, particularly cases against government decisions or actions. They ensure that administrative actions comply with legal standards.

2. **Labor Courts:** Specialized courts deal with labor disputes between employers and employees. These courts focus on issues such as labor rights, employment contracts, and collective bargaining.

3. **Electoral Courts:** The Electoral Tribunal of the Federal Judiciary oversees the legality of elections in Mexico. It adjudicates disputes related to electoral processes, ensuring compliance with electoral laws and regulations.

4. **Military Courts:** These courts address offenses committed by military personnel under the military justice system. They handle cases that involve military discipline and conduct.

5. **Juvenile Courts:** These courts focus on cases involving minors, particularly in matters of delinquency and protection. They aim to provide rehabilitative rather than punitive measures.

6. **Family Courts:** Specialized in family law matters, these courts handle cases related to divorce, child custody, adoption, and domestic violence, ensuring that family-related disputes are resolved appropriately.

---

48 https://lawlibrary.arizona.edu/mexican-legal-system

The Mexican judiciary has several distinctive features that set it apart. One notable aspect is the *amparo system,* which allows individuals to protect their constitutional rights by challenging laws or government actions they believe violate those rights. Recent judicial reforms have introduced an adversarial criminal justice system, emphasizing transparency and defendants' rights, allowing for greater participation in legal proceedings.

While the judiciary is constitutionally independent, it faces challenges such as political pressures and corruption, leading to ongoing efforts to strengthen this independence. There are initiatives aimed at enhancing the training and professionalization of judges and judicial personnel to improve legal education and promote best practices. Access to justice is another focus, with efforts to provide legal aid and resources for marginalized communities.

Additionally, the judiciary is increasingly integrating technology to streamline processes and enhance transparency, with digital platforms for filing cases and accessing court documents becoming more common. These elements reflect the dynamic and evolving nature of the judiciary in Mexico, highlighting both its challenges and advancements.

Some Fun Facts

- In October 2024, Mexico became the only legal system in the world where its judges would be elected by popular vote.[49]
- It's a law in Mexico that requires you to keep both feet on the pedals if you're on a bike. You could get arrested if you don't.[50]
- Regardless of whether you're a citizen or you're able to vote in a local election, is it illegal to drink alcohol within a 72-hour period leading up to any state or national election in Mexico.[51]

---

49 https://www.abc.net.au/news/2024-09-11/
mexico-becomes-first-country-to-approve-election-of-judges/

50 https://www.worldnomads.com/travel-safety/worldwide/
unexpected-laws-to-know-avoid-trouble-when-traveling

51 https://lawyerfrommexico.com/strange-laws-in-mexico/

General Questions

1. *Will the court treat first-time offenders and tourists with more leniency?* In Mexico, courts may show some leniency toward first-time offenders and tourists, particularly for minor offenses. Factors such as the nature of the offense, the individual's background, and whether they show remorse can influence a judge's decision. However, this leniency is not guaranteed and can vary significantly depending on the specific circumstances of each case and the applicable laws.

   Additionally, serious offenses are likely to be treated more harshly, regardless of the offender's status. It's essential for anyone in legal trouble to seek appropriate legal advice to navigate the system effectively.

2. *If I am charged with a crime, which court is likely to hear my case?* If you are charged with a crime in Mexico, your case will likely be heard in a criminal court. The specific court will depend on various factors, including the nature and severity of the offense. For minor offenses, it may be handled in a local or municipal court. For more serious crimes, it would typically go to a federal court or a state court, depending on whether the offense is under federal or state jurisdiction. If you're unsure about the specifics of your case, it's advisable to consult with a legal professional familiar with Mexican law.

3. *What is the standard of proof in a criminal case in Mexico?* In Mexico, the accused is considered guilty until proven innocent. The standard of proof in a criminal case is "beyond a reasonable doubt." This means that the prosecution must provide sufficient evidence to convince the judge of the defendant's guilt to a high degree of certainty. This standard is intended to ensure that any conviction is based on a strong evidentiary foundation; the burden of proof lies with the prosecution, which must establish the defendant's guilt through credible evidence and arguments.

4. *If I am arrested in Mexico, is pretrial detention mandatory?* **Yes.** Pre-trial detention is mandatory for many crimes and the criminal justice process can move very slowly.

5. *Are there jury trials in Mexico?* **No.** There are no jury trials in Mexico, in either civil or criminal court.

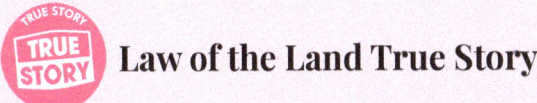

Law of the Land True Story

Probably the most notable high-profile criminal case in Mexico is the trial of Joaquín "El Chapo" Guzmán, the infamous leader of the Sinaloa drug cartel.

His trial took place in the United States, but it had profound effects on Mexico's judicial landscape, particularly concerning issues of corruption and the fight against organized crime.

Guzmán was captured multiple times and escaped from a prison in Mexico on two occasions. His criminal activities included large-scale drug trafficking, money laundering, and violent crimes. After his extradition to the U.S. in 2017, he faced trial in New York City.

The trial began in November 2018 and lasted several months. Prosecutors presented extensive evidence, including testimonies from former associates, intercepted communications, and financial records. Guzmán was charged with running a criminal enterprise responsible for smuggling vast quantities of drugs into the U.S., among other crimes.

In February 2019, Guzmán was found guilty on multiple counts, leading to a life sentence plus 30 years. The trial highlighted the challenges faced by the Mexican judiciary in dealing with organized crime and corruption, as Guzmán's cartel had significant influence over various aspects of Mexican society, including law enforcement and politics.

The trial underscored the need for judicial reforms in Mexico, particularly in the areas of protecting witnesses and combating corruption within the judicial system. It also sparked discussions about the effectiveness of the Mexican legal framework in addressing organized crime and the complexities of extradition processes between the U.S. and Mexico.

Takeaways

- Mexico follows a civil law system, emphasizing codified laws and statutes rather than judicial precedents. The Constitution and various legal codes form the foundation of the legal framework.

- The judiciary comprises multiple levels, including the Supreme Court, federal courts, and state courts, each handling different types of cases. The Supreme Court interprets the Constitution and ensures uniformity in the application of federal law.

- The amparo action is a unique feature that allows individuals to challenge government actions or laws that violate their constitutional rights, promoting judicial review and accountability.

- Legal proceedings often follow an inquisitorial model, where judges play an active role in investigating cases, contrasting with the adversarial system used in common law jurisdictions.

- The influence of organized crime poses serious challenges to the judiciary, highlighting the need for protective measures for judges, witnesses, and legal professionals involved in high-stakes cases.

CRIME VICTIM ASSISTANCE

CRIME VICTIM ASSISTANCE

Overview

Traveling to Mexico can be an enriching experience, however, like any destination, it is important for tourists to be aware of the potential risks associated with crime. While many visitors enjoy their trips without incident, it is crucial to recognize that crime can happen, and being informed can help mitigate its impact. Understanding the resources available for crime victim assistance is essential for ensuring safety and support during your visit.

Mexico has various resources to assist victims, including tourists who may find themselves in difficult situations.

Resources include:

- **Government Support:** The Mexican government has implemented laws, such as the General Law on Victims, aimed at protecting the rights of individuals affected by crime. This includes provisions for assistance, psychological support, and, in some cases, financial compensation. Tourists are encouraged to report any incidents to local authorities, who are obligated to provide guidance on available resources.

- **Emergency Contacts:** Tourists should familiarize themselves with emergency numbers in Mexico. For example, dialing 911 will connect you to local police, medical services, and fire departments. In case of a crime, it is advisable to file a report immediately to ensure that appropriate actions can be taken.

- **Non-Governmental Organizations (NGOs):** Various NGOs operate across Mexico, providing support specifically for crime victims. These organizations often offer legal advice, counseling, and assistance with navigating the local justice system. Many are equipped to help non-Mexican citizens and can be a valuable resource in time of need.

- **Consular Support:** Tourists can seek assistance from their home country's consulate or embassy in Mexico. Consulates can provide guidance, help with communication, and connect victims with local resources. They can also assist with replacing lost passports or other important documents.

While it's important to know where to seek help, preventive measures can greatly reduce the likelihood of encountering crime. Tourists are encouraged to stay informed about safe areas to visit, avoid displaying valuables, and remain aware of their surroundings. Engaging with reputable tour operators and avoiding risky situations can enhance safety during your trip.

 **What to Do If You Are the Victim of a Crime**

If you become a victim of a crime during your visit to Mexico, first and foremost, prioritize your safety by moving to a secure location and staying calm. As soon as possible, contact local authorities by dialing 911 for immediate assistance, and file a police report to document the incident, which may be necessary for insurance claims. If injured, seek medical attention right away, as hospitals can document your injuries for legal purposes. Also, reach out to your embassy or consulate for support, as they can provide legal advice and help navigate the local system.

U.S. Embassy Mexico City[52]
Paseo de la Reforma 305
Colonia Cuauhtemoc
06500 Ciudad de Mexico
Mexico

U.S. Citizen Services:
From Mexico 800-681-9374 or 55-8526-2561
From the United States 1-844-528-6611
Website: https://mx.usembassy.gov/contact/

Access victim assistance services through government programs and local NGOs that offer counseling and legal aid. Document everything related to the incident, including dates, times, and witness information, which can be helpful for the investigation. Notify your travel insurance provider about the incident to understand the claims process for any losses incurred. Lastly, stay informed by following up with authorities about your case and familiarizing yourself with your rights as a victim in Mexico. While such experiences can be distressing, knowing how to respond can help you manage the situation effectively.

Common Financial Scams in Mexico

In Mexico, like many other countries, tourists as well as locals can fall victim to various financial scams of varying degrees. Here are some common ones to be aware of:

1. **Fake Tour Operators:** Some individuals or companies offer tours at incredibly low prices but may provide subpar services or no services at all after payment. Do your due diligence and pick a trusted operator, even if it is a bit more expensive!

2. **Credit Card Skimming:** Scammers may use devices to capture credit card information at ATMs or during transactions at shops and restaurants.

---

52 For U.S. citizens

3. **Currency Exchange Scams:** Unscrupulous money changers may offer unfavorable rates or charge hidden fees, leading to less cash than expected.

4. **Rental Scams:** When looking for vacation rentals, be cautious of listings that ask for deposits without proper verification. Some may be fake or double-booked properties.

5. **Overcharging:** Especially in tourist areas, some vendors may inflate prices or charge tourists more than locals for the same goods or services.

6. **ATM Scams:** Some ATMs may have added devices that capture card information. Always use machines located in well-lit, secure areas, preferably inside banks.

7. **Fake Police Officers:** Scammers may pose as police officers, claiming you're involved in illegal activity and demanding cash for "fines" or bribes.

8. **Investment Scams:** Promises of high returns on investments in real estate or business ventures can be enticing, but many are fraudulent schemes.

9. **Romance Scams:** Online scammers may build relationships with victims, eventually asking for money to cover supposed emergencies or travel expenses.

10. **Lottery or Prize Scams:** Victims may receive messages claiming they've won a lottery or prize but must pay a fee to claim it.

 **Some Safety Recommendations**

Be cautious of deals that seem too good to be true, especially if they involve significantly lower prices. Scammers often pressure you to act quickly, claiming that an offer is only available for a limited time. If a tour operator or service provider cannot provide legitimate contact information or verifiable credentials, that's a warning sign.

Watch for poor communication, especially if responses are vague or unclear regarding pricing and services. Requests for cash payments instead of credit cards or invoices can also be suspicious, as scammers prefer cash to avoid tracking. Unprofessional behavior, such as disorganization or lack of identification, can further indicate a scam.

High-pressure sales tactics, especially if someone is overly aggressive in trying to sell you something, should raise concern. When using ATMs, look for signs of tampering and use machines in well-lit areas. Be wary if a service provider refuses to provide a written agreement or receipt, and if you receive inconsistent information from different people, it's best to be skeptical. Staying alert to these signs can help protect you from potential scams.

Sexual Assault

If you experience sexual violence in Mexico, prioritize your safety first. Call 911 from any phone to reach local police or request medical assistance. Seek help at a hospital or health center and contact your embassy.

Reporting sexual violence in Mexico differs from the process in the U.S. While the U.S. Embassy can offer support, it's best to consult a local lawyer for legal advice. You must file a police report in person at the local Prosecutor's Office (*Ministerio Público*) within 72 hours to preserve evidence. The Public Prosecutor's Office will provide protective measures for victims, investigate the case, and keep you updated on its status. You may be referred to a specialized unit for sexual violence cases, and the process can take several hours.

If you need language assistance, you have the right to request a translator or interpreter. Your police report will be written in Spanish, so review it carefully before signing. The prosecutor's office may also request your consent for medical examinations and psychological evaluations, which are free and can be conducted by professionals you trust.

If you choose to file a report, do so before leaving Mexico. Once the report is complete, you can appoint someone with power of attorney to act on your behalf while you return home. However, you may still be required to return to Mexico at various stages of the legal process. Keep in mind that trials can last over a year, depending on various factors. For minors, a police report is also required, and they must be accompanied by a parent or legal guardian. Local authorities are responsible for following laws regarding minors. (https://canadainmexico.com/wp-content/uploads/2021/11/SGBV-En-Digital.pdf)

What are your rights as a victim of sexual violence in Mexico?

You are entitled to be treated with respect and to have your personal information kept confidential. Authorities are obligated to provide you with effective protection, and you can file a report either alone or with someone you trust.

You have the right to receive medical and psychological care at any public health center or hospital without needing to file a police report. Additionally, you should be given clear and accurate information to help you make informed decisions about your care options.

You can access free and expedited legal advice and, if needed, request an interpreter or translator at no cost if you don't speak Spanish. Foreigners are also entitled to consular assistance. Lastly, you should be able to pursue justice in a timely manner, free from gender-related stereotypes.

 **Some Safety Recommendations**

- Be mindful of your surroundings and avoid distractions like excessive phone use.
- If something feels wrong or makes you uncomfortable, leave the situation.
- Whenever possible, go out with friends or trusted individuals.

- Choose reputable taxis or rideshare services instead of accepting rides from strangers.
- Be aware of your alcohol and substance consumption to maintain control over your situation.
- Communicate your boundaries assertively and be firm if someone crosses them.
- Familiarize yourself with local emergency numbers and resources available for support.
- Know safe places you can go and have a plan for how to get there if needed.

Consular Assistance

U.S. embassies and consulates offer essential support to victims of crime abroad by addressing emergency needs arising from the incident and facilitating access to appropriate medical care. They provide guidance on how to report the crime to local law enforcement and may accompany victims to the police station when possible. Additionally, they assist in obtaining updates about the legal case from local authorities and help replace lost or stolen passports.

Embassies also connect victims with resources both overseas and in the U.S., explain financial assistance options for returning home, and assist with travel arrangements. They can contact designated individuals in the U.S. while adhering to privacy regulations.

The resources available can vary by location, but the nearest U.S. embassy or consulate can provide information about local doctors, counselors, and legal professionals to help victims after a crime. Timely medical treatment is crucial, particularly after certain incidents. The embassy can inform you about medical options and associated costs in the host country, including care for sexually transmitted infections or unwanted pregnancies. In serious cases like sexual assault, a forensic exam may be necessary to collect evidence for prosecution, ideally conducted within 72 hours after the incident.

However, keep in mind the U.S. embassy or consulate does not cover legal, medical, or other expenses for victims of crime. Additionally, consular officers are unable to investigate crimes, offer legal advice, or act as official interpreters or translators.[53]

 ## General Questions

1. *If I am a victim of a crime, can I legally be compensated?* **Yes**, as a victim of a crime in Mexico, you may be entitled to compensation under certain circumstances. The legal framework allows victims to seek reparations, which can include financial compensation for damages, medical expenses, and other related costs. To pursue compensation, you typically need to file a report with local authorities and may also need to initiate a civil claim against the perpetrator.

   It's advisable to consult with a local attorney who specializes in victim rights or personal injury law to understand the specific processes and options available to you. Additionally, various organizations may offer assistance in navigating the legal system and seeking compensation.

2. *If a family member falls victim to homicide, can I bring the body back to my home country?* **Yes**, if a family member falls victim to homicide, you can typically bring the body back to your home country, but the process can be complex and may involve several steps. You will need to coordinate with local authorities in Mexico to obtain the necessary permits and documentation for repatriation.

   The steps usually include:

---

53 https://travel.state.gov/content/dam/NEWTravelAssets/pdfs/Crime%20 Victim%20Assistance_Brochure

1. **Death Certificate:** Obtain an official death certificate from local authorities.

2. **Autopsy and Investigation:** If an autopsy is required or an investigation is ongoing, there may be delays.

3. **Funeral Home Services:** Work with a local funeral home that specializes in repatriation. They can assist with embalming, necessary paperwork, and logistics.

4. **Embassy/Consulate Assistance:** Contact your country's embassy or consulate in Mexico for guidance and support throughout the process.

5. **Transportation Arrangements:** Coordinate with airlines and ensure that all necessary regulations are met for transporting human remains.

It's advisable to start the process as soon as possible and to seek legal or logistical help to navigate any challenges.

3. *If a family member falls victim to homicide, will I receive any assistance from the Mexican government?* If a family member falls victim to homicide in Mexico, you may receive assistance from the Mexican government, though the level of support can vary. Victim assistance programs are available, providing counseling, legal guidance, and information about navigating the legal process. Some states also offer compensation programs for victims of violent crimes, which may cover funeral expenses and other costs, although eligibility and application procedures differ by state. Additionally, local NGOs and community organizations may offer emotional support and help with bureaucratic processes. It's advisable to contact local authorities, your country's embassy or consulate, and relevant NGOs for guidance during this challenging time.

POLICE

POLICE

Overview

As the statistics attest, the police force in Mexico is significantly understaffed, overworked (and underpaid). Mexico has an average around 230 officers per 100,000 residents, but the number of police officers varies by region, with Mexico City having the highest rate and Tamaulipas having the lowest.[54] An analysis conducted by the National Public Security System (SNSP) identified that there were 123,070 state police officers in Mexico's 32 federal entities at the end of 2020, equivalent to 0.96 state police officers per 1,000 residents.[55]

Understaffing is one of several challenges facing the Mexican police, whose reliability varies significantly by region. While some areas have effective officers, others struggle with issues like corruption, inadequate training, and resource shortages, which contribute to low public trust, especially in high-crime areas. The police image is mixed; in some regions, they are seen as crucial for safety, while in others, distrust arises from corruption and abuse. Despite this, many dedicated officers work to improve community safety and rebuild trust, with ongoing reform efforts aimed at enhancing police accountability and public perception.

---

54 https://insightcrime.org/news/brief/
mexico-police-are-overworked-underpaid-and-poorly-distributed-report/

55 https://mexiconewsdaily.com/news/

Police Response

Police in Mexico have several key roles and responsibilities. They engage in crime prevention through patrols, community outreach, and various programs. Investigative units focus on serious crimes, gathering evidence and conducting inquiries. Additionally, police are responsible for public safety, responding to emergencies, managing public events, and maintaining peace during protests.

However, the police face significant challenges. Corruption is a pervasive issue that leads to widespread distrust in police institutions, prompting efforts to improve training and oversight. High levels of violence from organized crime also pose risks to both police officers and the communities they serve, often resulting in threats and attacks. Furthermore, allegations of human rights abuses, such as extrajudicial killings and torture, significantly impact the legitimacy of the police.

To address these issues, initiatives aimed at community policing have been implemented to foster trust between law enforcement and the public, encouraging collaboration to solve local problems. Various governments have also undertaken reform efforts to enhance police accountability, training, and operational efficiency, including new protocols and increased transparency. In areas with high crime rates, police frequently collaborate with military forces to bolster security and combat organized crime.

 **Structure of Mexican Police**

Mexican police operate through a multi-tiered structure that includes federal, state, and municipal forces, each with distinct responsibilities and challenges.

Federal Level:

Mexico has two primary federal law enforcement agencies: the National Guard, a uniformed paramilitary force, and the Ministerial Federal Police (Policía Federal Ministerial, PFM), which serves as the investigative arm of the Attorney General.

The National Guard oversees federal law enforcement and public security. It was formed to address organized crime and improve coordination among various agencies, whereas the Federal Ministerial Police focuses on investigations related to federal crimes.

In addition, in Mexico City as a federal district, the Secretariat of Public Security oversees a large police force of over 90,000 officers, responsible for maintaining public order. The city also has its own investigative Judicial Police organized under the local Attorney General's office, along with specialized units like the Traffic Police, which is the largest single law enforcement body in Mexico. Other agencies, such as the Mexican Immigration Service and customs officers from the Secretariat of Finance, also play roles in law enforcement, focusing on immigration control and contraband interdiction, respectively. The Bank of Mexico has its security division to enforce banking laws and combat financial crimes.[56]

State Level:

Each of Mexico's thirty-one states has both preventive and judicial police, collectively referred to as the State Judicial Police. These state police forces operate under the authority of the state's governor. The line between crimes investigated by State and Federal Judicial Police can be ambiguous; most offenses fall under state jurisdiction, while federal police handle drug trafficking, crimes against the government, and offenses that cross multiple jurisdictions. State-level preventive police forces number around 90,000, while the state-level judicial police comprise about 25,000 officers.

State police (Policía Estatal) operate from precinct stations known as delegaciones, with each delegación typically staffed by around 200

---

56 https://en.wikipedia.org/wiki/Federal_Police_(Mexico)

officers. The highest-ranking officer is called a comandante, similar to a first captain in the military, with the remaining personnel holding ranks such as first sergeant, second sergeant, and corporal.[57]

Municipal Level:

In Mexico, some municipalities have their own police forces, known as Policía Municipal, tasked with managing minor civil disturbances and traffic violations that are also often the first point of contact for citizens.

Out of the 2,457 municipalities, 650 do not have police forces. Nevertheless, some of these municipal forces are significant and well-equipped.

---

57 https://en.wikipedia.org/wiki/Law_enforcement_in_Mexico

HOW TO GET LEGAL HELP IN MEXICO

- Available Resources
- Legal Aid
- Foreign Embassies in Mexico

CHAPTER 16

HOW TO GET LEGAL HELP IN MEXICO

Available Resources

If you find yourself in legal trouble in Mexico, the first step is to contact the nearest embassy or consulate immediately. They can provide a list of local English-speaking attorneys, visit you if you're detained, and help you navigate the local legal system, although they cannot offer legal advice.

Key actions include informing the embassy about your situation, especially if you've been arrested, and asking for a lawyer referral. Once you have a lawyer, consult them for guidance and representation regarding your legal issue. It's important to understand that you have certain rights if arrested. You have the right to remain silent and not answer questions without a lawyer present. You are entitled to legal representation, which means you can request a lawyer of your choice or have one provided by the state if you cannot afford one. You must be informed of the charges against you clearly and promptly. If you are a foreign national, you have the right to contact your consulate or embassy for assistance. You are entitled to humane treatment and protection from torture or mistreatment while in custody. If you require medical assistance, you have the right to receive it. Additionally, you have the right to notify a family member or a third party about your arrest.

Emergency Assistance For U.S. Citizens In Mexico

From Mexico: 800-681-9374 or 55-8526-2561

From the United States: 1-844-528-6611

https://mx.usembassy.gov/

Legal Aid

Keep in mind potential language barriers; hiring an English-speaking lawyer is advisable if you are not fluent in Spanish. The legal processes in Mexico may differ from those in the U.S. and elsewhere, so it's crucial to consult someone familiar with the local system. Additionally, some non-profit organizations may offer free legal assistance for certain cases.

To find a reliable lawyer in Mexico, start by checking the U.S. Consulate's online list of attorneys, organized by consular district.[58] You can also explore platforms like LinkedIn, chambers of commerce, industry associations, and trade organizations for potential lawyers. Other useful resources include legal directories, law lists, and targeted Google searches.

Once you have a list of candidates, conduct thorough due diligence by verifying their credentials, checking references and past cases, and looking into their involvement in lawsuits. Ensure they specialize in the relevant area of law and have a strong track record of success in similar cases. Martindale-Hubbell and its sister site, Lawyers.com, are highly regarded legal directories that can serve as excellent starting points for your search.

Foreign Embassies in Mexico

Embassies and consulates in Mexico fulfill several important roles. The U.S. Embassy in Mexico City represents the U.S. government in political, economic, and public diplomacy matters. Consulates provide various consular services, such as assistance with immigration and

---

58 https://mx.usembassy.gov/find-your-consular-location/

emergencies; for instance, the U.S. Consulate General in Tijuana has a Vehicle Recovery Unit to help citizens recover stolen vehicles. They also process a range of visas, including nonimmigrant, immigrant, and K-1 fiancé(e) visas.

Additionally, the U.S. Embassy manages security assistance programs from the Department of Defense, which include training and technical support for the military. The Department of Justice Attaché's Office in Mexico addresses legal assistance issues and coordinates extradition processes. Consulates, like the one in Ciudad Juarez, also work to strengthen bilateral relations between the U.S. and Mexico.

Most foreign embassies and consulates in Mexico are located in Mexico City, with many concentrated along the Paseo de la Reforma corridor and around Chapultepec Park. However, some countries have set up shop in other areas, such as Lomas de Chapultepec. Mexico City is home to about 85 embassies from countries around the world.[59]

*U.S. Embassies and Consulates in Mexico

Mexico City (Principal Office)

Paseo de la Reforma 305
Colonia Cuahtemoc, Mexico D.F.
C.P. 06500
Telephone: +52 55 5080-2000
Website: www.usembassy-mexico.gov

Guadalajara

Progreso 175
Col. Americana
Guadalajara, Jalisco, Mexico
C.P. 44160
Telephone: +52 33 3268-2100
Website: http://guadalajara.usconsulate.gov/

---

59 https://mexicocity.cdmx.gob.mx/category/embassies/

Monterrey

U.S. Consulate General
150 Prolongacion Avenida Alfonso Reyes
69196 Santa Catarina, N.L.
Telephone: +52 81 8047-3100
Website: http://monterrey.usconsulate.gov/

 You can look for your country's embassy or consulate at **https://mx.usembassy.gov/ find-your-consular-location/.**

MEDICAL FACILITIES & HOSPITALS

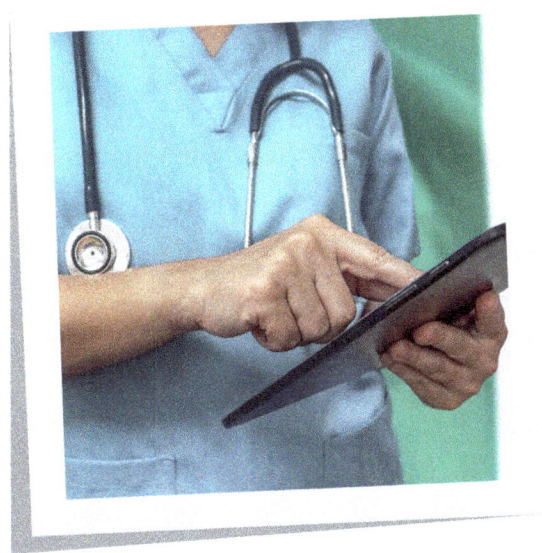

CHAPTER 17

MEDICAL FACILITIES & HOSPITALS

Overview

The healthcare system in Mexico is generally efficient and offers good standards, particularly in large cities with excellent hospitals and clinics. Healthcare is affordable, and many Mexican doctors receive training in the U.S. or Europe, resulting in a high number of English-speaking physicians. However, a significant portion of the population can only access basic care, and Mexico has one of the lowest per capita healthcare expenditures among OECD countries.[60]

Mexico's healthcare system operates on a three-tier model: the IMSS, which covers employees in the private and public sectors; Seguro Popular, which provides coverage for those who don't qualify for IMSS; and private insurance, which offers more comfort and privacy but is expensive. Eligibility for IMSS typically requires formal employment, though voluntary enrollment is available for legal residents, including expats.

Healthcare costs in Mexico are relatively low, with a doctor's visit averaging around 400 pesos (about $20 USD), and diagnostic tests often costing significantly less than in the U.S. However, costs can rise for complicated procedures, especially in tourist areas where prices may be inflated. There's a noticeable quality gap between rural and urban care, with private facilities offering shorter wait times and better amenities.

---

60 https://www.oecd.org/en.html

For expats, IMSS provides comprehensive coverage at a low cost, but it excludes pre-existing conditions. Thus, private insurance may be more suitable for those with existing health issues. Tourists should obtain travel medical insurance since they are not eligible for public health insurance and may need to pay upfront for services.

Pharmacies in Mexico are categorized into two types: Segunda Clase, which sell common medications but not regulated drugs, and Primera Clase, which can sell any medication prescribed by a doctor, including controlled substances. It's advisable to be aware of these distinctions when seeking medication.[61]

When traveling to Mexico, it's important to understand that while good healthcare is available, most hospitals require upfront payment, particularly for non-residents, and U.S. health insurance is generally not accepted. Therefore, purchasing travel insurance with medical coverage is highly recommended, as the quality of care can vary widely between facilities. Mexico has a dual healthcare system: a public system (IMSS) for citizens and residents, and a private system that typically offers better quality and faster service but at a higher cost. Additionally, while some medical staff may speak English, not all do, so knowing basic Spanish phrases can be helpful. To avoid high out-of-pocket expenses for medical emergencies, consider travel insurance before your trip. If you prefer faster service and potentially higher quality care, private healthcare facilities are a better option.

Emergency Numbers in Mexico

 In the event of any emergency, dial 911.

911 is Mexico's national emergency number; the service is answered and attended to locally and will give you the fastest response.

---

61 https://www.internationalinsurance.com/health/systems/mexico.php

For non-emergency situations in Mexico City, you can call LOCATEL at 55-5658-1111. Operators are available to assist with any non-life-threatening issues.

Additionally, for tourist-related concerns, you can reach the Tourist Assistance Hotline at 55-5286-7097 or 55-5286-9077. The service is available Monday through Friday from 9 a.m. to 6 p.m. This hotline can help with issues specific to your trip, including communication with your embassy, visa-related inquiries, and airport transport concerns.[62]

Hospital Locations

Mexico's healthcare system features more than 5,000 hospitals, with an increase of over 600 facilities in the past decade. The majority of these hospitals are private and for-profit, including many of the country's top-ranked institutions. In 2021, the total number of hospital employees rose to 926,860, up from about 899,230 the year before. (https://www.statista.com/statistics/287090/number-of-hospitals-in-mexico/)

Cities with Best Medical Care

Mexico City is home to the finest hospitals in the country. According to Newsweek's 2024 Best Hospitals list, 10 out of the top 12 hospitals in Mexico are located in and around Mexico City. Additionally, Guadalajara and Monterrey also feature among the top 10 hospitals in the country.

Top Hospitals for International Visitors

Here are the best hospitals in Mexico, featuring both public and private options. All are located in Mexico City and provide state-of-the-art facilities along with high-quality patient care. The private hospitals listed are particularly recognized for their concierge services tailored for international patients. Many of these facilities are accredited by the Joint

---

62 https://mexicocity.cdmx.gob.mx/e/emergency/

Commission International (JCI), a non-profit organization based in the United States that assesses quality and safety in healthcare.

*It's worth noting that while the IMSS website is not available in English, there is typically at least one bilingual staff member on hand, especially at facilities in the capital.

Best Private Hospitals:[63]

1. Hospital Medica Sur

Puente de Piedra 150, Toriello Guerra, Tlalpan, 14050 Ciudad de México, CDMX, Mexico

Phone: +52 55 5424 7200

Whatsapp: +52 55 4635 5605

Email: miuriber@medicasur.org.mx

Hospital Médica Sur currently tops Newsweek's 2024 Best Hospitals in Mexico list and has been one of Mexico's best hospitals for over a decade. The hospital works together with the Mayo Clinic, one of the leading hospitals in the United States. A popular choice for medical tourism, Médica Sur has dedicated staff to support expats before, during and after their stay.

2. Centro Médico ABC

Campus Santa Fe: Av. Carlos Graef Fernández 154, Col. Santa Fe, Cuajimalpa, 05300, Ciudad de México, Mexico

Phone: +52 55 1103 1680

Email: atnpubsf@abchospital.com Campus Observatorio: Sur 136 No. 116, Col. Las Américas, Álvaro Obregón, 01120, Ciudad de México, Mexico

Phone: +52 55 5230-8880

Email: atencionalpublico@abchospital.com

---

63 https://www.internationalinsurance.com/hospitals/mexico/

Centro Médico ABC has two different campuses that are both rated among the top five best hospitals in Mexico. ABC has been associated with Houston Methodist Hospital since 2006. They are JCI-accredited and have, among other services, one of the most advanced cancer centers in Latin America. As a non-profit organization, the hospital invests extra funding back into vulnerable communities through specialized care, teaching and research.

3.Hospitales Ángeles – Lomas

Vialidad de la Barranca s/n, Hacienda de las Palmas, 52763 Huixquilucan, Mexico
Phone: +52 55 5246 5000

Hospital Angeles is a privately owned chain of hospitals in Latin America. The hospitals are known for their state-of-the-art technology and patient-centered care. They offer concierge services for international patients and are a popular site for medical tourism. The Lomas campus is a ten-story building with 175 medical offices.

Best Public Hospitals:

1. IMSS – Centro Médico Nacional Siglo XXI

Av. Cuauhtémoc 330, Doctores, Cuauhtémoc, 06720 Ciudad de México, CDMX, Mexico
Phone: +52 55 5627 6900

Centro Médico Nacional Siglo XXI is a public hospital complex managed by the Mexican Social Security Institute (IMSS). It is the best IMSS hospital in the country and specializes in cardiology, oncology and pediatrics.

2. IMSS – Centro Médico Nacional La Raza

P.º de las Jacarandas S/N, La Raza, Azcapotzalco, 02990 Ciudad de México, CDMX, Mexico
Phone: +52 800 623 2323

Centro Médico Nacional La Raza is another public hospital managed by the IMSS. It's a research hospital and a pioneer in specialized transplants, best known for its bone marrow transplant center.

Is there an American Hospital in Mexico?

Numerous Mexican hospitals have affiliations with American hospitals and healthcare organizations. The most well-known among them, The Amerimed Hospital Group, focuses on medical tourism and adheres to U.S. care standards. Their facilities are located in popular tourist areas such as Playa del Carmen, Cancun, and Cozumel.

 For highly regarded hospitals in other parts of Mexico, please visit **https://www.internationalinsurance.com/ hospitals/mexico/**.

Medical Emergencies

What should I do if I feel unwell/sick in Mexico?

Mexico offers both public and private hospitals for expats and visitors. If you are legally employed and paying taxes in the country, your employer should automatically enroll you in the public IMSS insurance program. Self-employed individuals can also register, provided they hold a valid residency permit.

However, if you're just a tourist, you may pay out-of-pocket. Hospitals in Mexico generally require payment upfront for services rendered and will place holds on credit cards if a patient is admitted. The U.S. Government does not pay for medical care overseas. Some private U.S. insurance companies pay for medical care overseas, but usually on a reimbursable basis, meaning that you will need to pay first and request reimbursement later. Patients should contact their insurance company as soon as possible to understand exactly what services the insurance company will cover.

What If I Need Hospital Care in Mexico?

While IMSS hospitals have skilled doctors who deliver quality care, many foreigners prefer the private healthcare system. Private hospitals typically offer shorter wait times, a broader selection of specialists, and more advanced medical technology.

If you require treatment for an injury or need surgery, private hospitals usually allow you to book appointments directly with a doctor through their websites, many of which are available in English. Some facilities even provide concierge services for international patients, particularly those seeking medical care while visiting Mexico. It is advisable for expats and travelers alike to invest in a comprehensive international health insurance plan to cover any potential medical expenses while abroad.

 **Insurance Guidance**

In most instances, you cannot use American insurance for treatments in Mexico. Hospitals in Mexico typically do not have reciprocal agreements with other countries, and American plans like Medicare or Medicaid are not accepted. If you are not eligible for the IMSS program, you will have to rely on the private healthcare system. Consequently, many expats choose to buy global health insurance plans to ensure they are covered while in Mexico.

Healthcare costs in Mexico can vary significantly based on the hospital, the specific illness, the location, and other factors. Interestingly, the average cost for a doctor's visit is comparable to that of an emergency room visit, typically ranging from $15 to $20 USD. However, be aware that some facilities in areas with large foreign populations may charge higher rates. Most Mexican healthcare providers do not offer direct billing, so you will need to pay for services upfront. Afterward, you can submit the necessary paperwork to your insurance for reimbursement.

DRIVING IN MEXICO

- Overview
- Main Traffic Rules
- Road Safety
- General Questions
- Law of the Land Hypothetical

DRIVING IN MEXICO

Overview

Driving in Mexico offers a blend of stunning scenery, diverse road conditions, and unique local driving customs. Major highways, known as "cuotas," are generally well-maintained toll roads that provide safer and faster travel. In contrast, "libre" roads are free to use but can be in poorer condition and have more traffic. Urban areas often experience congestion, and road conditions can vary significantly.

Speed limits are usually posted, with urban areas having lower limits around 40 km/h (approximately 25 m/h), while highways allow speeds up to 110 km/h (about 70 m/h). Seatbelts are mandatory for all passengers, and there are strict DUI laws, with a limit of 0.08% in most states; however, it's safest to avoid drinking altogether if you plan to drive.

Driving in Mexico can be aggressive, with behaviors like tailgating and rapid lane changes being common occurrences, so defensive driving is advisable. In roundabouts, you should yield to traffic already in the circle, and be cautious of pedestrians, who may cross unexpectedly.

Having adequate insurance coverage is essential, as many U.S. policies do not extend to Mexico. It's also advisable to have a roadside assistance plan for emergencies, as help may not be readily available. Many travelers recommend avoiding driving at night due to safety concerns.

Navigation is best done with a combination of GPS and physical maps, as access to mobile data can be unreliable, especially in rural areas. When driving, ensure you have all necessary documentation, including your driver's license, vehicle registration, and insurance. While an International Driving Permit (IDP) is not mandatory, it can facilitate communication with authorities.

 **Things to know before driving in Mexico**

- When driving in Mexico, you can use a U.S. license, a license in English or Spanish, or an International Driver's License.

- It's crucial to have valid auto insurance specific to Mexico, as U.S. policies are not accepted; you can buy this insurance before your trip.

- Traffic violations often result in on-the-spot fines, so carrying cash is advisable.

- The legal blood alcohol limit is 0.08%, and driving under the influence is strictly prohibited.

- Turn signals can mean different things, such as a left signal indicating it's safe to pass. Be prepared for oncoming drivers to enter your lane to overtake others and expect to move over as needed.

- Many roads may have large potholes, and livestock can wander onto roads, requiring extra caution.

- Most highways are toll roads, and you can use a "toll card" for convenient payment. If traveling more than 12 miles into Mexico, you'll need to obtain TVIP and FMM cards. Additionally, Mexico City has a "No Driving Today" law that restricts certain vehicles on specific days.

 **Main Traffic Rules**[64]

- **Driving side:** Vehicles drive on the right-hand side of the road.

- **Speed limits:** Speed limits are in kilometers per hour and vary by location and road type. Signs along the road indicate the speed limit.

- **Traffic signals:** Drivers must obey traffic signals, signs, and road markings.

- **Seat belts:** All passengers, including those in the back seat, must wear a seat belt.

- **Alcohol:** Driving under the influence of alcohol or drugs is illegal, with a legal blood alcohol content limit of 0.08%.

- **Mobile devices:** Using a mobile device without a hands-free system is prohibited while driving.

- **Yielding:** Vehicles must yield to pedestrians at crosswalks. At intersections without traffic signals or signs, the vehicle on the right has the right of way.

- **Toll roads:** Toll roads, also known as "cuota" roads, are generally safer than free roads, also known as "libre" roads.

- **Oncoming vehicles:** Flashing headlights from an oncoming vehicle indicate that you should slow down. The first vehicle to flash has the right of way.

- **Slow-moving vehicles:** When approaching a slow-moving vehicle, it's customary for the slower vehicle to move to the shoulder to let you pass.

- **If stopped by police:** Remain calm and show the officer your proof of insurance, driver's license, and passport.

---

64 https://www.sixt.co.uk/magazine/tips/driving-tips-in-mexico

Road Safety

Traffic accidents are a significant problem in Mexico. They are a leading cause of death, particularly among young people aged 15 to 29. In fact, Mexico ranks seventh in the world in traffic fatalities, due to inadequate infrastructure, high-volume traffic, aggressive driving culture, poor enforcement of traffic laws, and a significant presence of vulnerable road users (pedestrians and cyclists) in addition to animal presence in the roads.[65]

To stay safe while driving in Mexico, consider the tips below:

- **Stay on main roads:** Stick to the main thoroughfares and avoid back roads. Toll roads, or "cuotas," are better maintained and safer than free roads.

- **Drive during daylight:** driving at night in Mexico is risky due to poor road conditions, inadequate lighting, and a higher likelihood of encountering reckless or impaired drivers, as well as wildlife in rural areas. There are also increased safety concerns related to crime, such as theft and carjackings.

- **Be aware of your surroundings:** Watch for pedestrians, carts, and bicycles that tend to wander into the streets and roads.

- **Understand traffic circles:** Learn how to navigate traffic circles and roundabouts.

- **Use turn signals correctly:** Understand that turn signals may be used for different purposes.

- **Have pesos:** Tollbooths in Mexico don't usually accept U.S. dollars, debit cards, or credit cards.

- **Have a plan if you get lost:** If you get lost, pull over and try to orient yourself.

- **Follow the rules of the road:** In Mexico, you drive on the right-hand side of the road and overtake on the left. Remember that seat belts are mandatory for all occupants.

---

65 https://www.intertraffic.com/news/
mexico-needs-better-and-safer-road-infrastructure

 **General Questions**

1. ***Can I use my driver's license from my home country to drive in Mexico?*** **Yes**, you can use your driver's license from your home country to drive in Mexico if it's written in English or Spanish. However, you may also need an International Driving Permit (IDP) that translates your identifying information into different languages.[66]

2. ***What is the age requirement for renting a car in Mexico?*** The minimum age to rent a car in Mexico is 18. Renters between 18 and 24 are charged an additional fee. The customer must also present a driver's license issued by the country of residence; the license must be issued by the same state entity as the official identification. [67]

 **Law of the Land Hypothetical**

HYPOTHETICAL: *Gwen, a tourist from Canada, is planning a two-week trip to Mexico. She wants to rent a car to explore the countryside but is unsure about the driving rules and whether her Canadian driver's license will be accepted. She also wonders if she should purchase additional insurance. Can she use her Canadian driver's license to rent a car in Mexico, and does she need to get extra insurance?*

ANSWER: *Yes, Gwen can use her Canadian driver's license to rent a car in Mexico—if it's valid and in English. However, it's recommended to obtain an International Driving Permit (IDP) for ease of*

---

66 https://www.usa.gov/international-drivers-license

67 https://www.hertzmexico.com/en/conditions/

communication, as some rental agencies may require it. As for insurance, basic coverage is typically included with rental cars, but it's wise to purchase additional insurance for comprehensive coverage, including liability and collision, to protect yourself against potential risks while driving in Mexico.

 **For more information on how to obtain IDP,** please visit **https://internationaldrivingpermit.org/how-to-apply/.**

NUDE BEACHES & CLOTHING-OPTIONAL RESORTS

NUDE BEACHES & CLOTHING-OPTIONAL RESORTS

Overview

Mexico, with its rich culture, history, warm climate and idyllic beaches, stretching along stunning coastline, attracts millions of tourists each year.

For those interested in embracing the naturist lifestyle and enjoying the country's natural beauty in the nude, it's essential to be aware of Mexico's public nudity laws, particularly regarding nudist beaches.

In Mexico, public nudity is not widely accepted and is considered a violation of the peace under the *Federal Penal Code*.[68] It is viewed as disrespectful to local customs and can potentially result in fines or detention. However, there are specific designated areas and nudist beaches where naturism is welcomed and embraced.

Many nude beaches are situated in remote or less-developed areas, offering privacy and a sense of escape from crowded tourist spots. Some beaches have gained official recognition as clothing-optional, which legitimizes nudism in the region and encourages more people to participate without fear of judgment.

---

68 https://www.beachatlas.com/nudism-laws-mexico

Mexico's first and only "legal" nude beach is *Zipolite*, located in Oaxaca on the southern Pacific coast. This long, golden sand beach is internationally recognized as a nudist haven and hosts the annual festival *Nudista Zipolite*, attracting nudists from around the world.

Playa del Secreto in the Riviera Maya and *Playa Sonrisa* on the Costa Maya are two other beaches where nudism is typically accepted. While not officially designated as nudist beaches, they are often less crowded and more secluded, providing a peaceful spot for naturists. There are other beaches that may permit nudity; however, it is advised to always conduct thorough research about the specific beach you plan to visit to keep your nudist experience enjoyable and trouble-free.

In addition, there are a number of hotels and resorts that boast small private beaches catering to nudism and naturism, such as *Punta Serena* in Jalisco, *Azulik* in Tulum, and *Hidden Beach Resort* near Xpu-Ha. These are all excellent choices for experiencing this lifestyle on your vacation in Mexico.

When visiting these beaches, it's important to remember and respect naturist etiquette. Always bring a towel to sit on, avoid taking photographs without explicit permission, and refrain from overtly sexual behavior which may be offensive to other beachgoers.

Legality and Safety

As stated above, the view of nudity in Mexico varies by location. While there are no federal laws specifically prohibiting nudism, naturists should be mindful of local regulations and cultural attitudes toward public nudity since it can be construed as "immoral" and is thus punishable at the discretion of local authorities. Certain states and municipalities may have their own restrictions, especially in more conservative areas.

However, in more liberal touristy areas, nudity is widely accepted. Many beaches and resorts have designated areas where nudism is welcomed and even encouraged. It's important to respect local customs and regulations, as well as the rules of specific establishments. Therefore, it's crucial to research and adhere to the rules of the specific region you intend to visit.

Nudist beaches and resorts in Mexico are often well-regarded for their welcoming environments and emphasis on respect and privacy. Popular spots, particularly in areas known for naturism, tend to attract like-minded individuals, creating a relaxed and safe atmosphere.

 ## Key Factors in Safety

However, safety can vary by location, so it's important to consider a few key factors:

1. **Research the Destination:** Look for established nudist beaches or resorts with good reviews. Online forums and social media can provide insights from fellow travelers about safety and experiences.

2. **Local Regulations:** Familiarize yourself with the rules of the specific beach or resort. Some places may have designated areas for nudism, while others might be more lenient. Adhering to local customs helps ensure a positive experience.

3. **Travel in Groups:** If possible, visit with friends or fellow travelers. There's safety in numbers, and it can enhance the experience to share it with others.

4. **Stay Aware of Your Surroundings:** As with any beach or resort, it's wise to be aware of your environment. Keep personal belongings secure and be cautious of anyone acting suspiciously.

5. **Trust Your Instincts:** If a place feels uncomfortable or unwelcoming, it's okay to leave and seek another location.

6. **Respect Others' Privacy:** Nudist communities value consent and privacy. Always be respectful of others and avoid taking photos without permission.

General Questions

1. *Are there specific beaches in Mexico that are well-known for nudism, and what should I know before visiting them?* Yes, Mexico has several well-known nudist beaches, such as *Playa Zipolite* in Oaxaca and *Playa de la Naturaleza* in Tulum. Before visiting, it's important to be aware of the local customs and regulations regarding nudity. Make sure to respect the beach's guidelines, such as keeping a respectful distance from others and refraining from photography without consent. Additionally, bring essentials like sunscreen, a towel, and water, as amenities can vary. Being open-minded and respectful will enhance your experience at these unique destinations.

2. *What should I wear when visiting a nude beach in Mexico, and is it necessary to bring anything specific?* When visiting a nude beach in Mexico, it's best to start with minimal clothing, like a swimsuit or cover-up, until you feel comfortable disrobing. Many people wear flip-flops or sandals for walking on hot sand. In addition to your towel, you should consider bringing essentials like sunscreen to protect your skin, especially for areas that may not be used to sun exposure. A hat and sunglasses can help shield your face and eyes from the sun. Staying hydrated is important, so bring water as well. A beach bag is useful for storing your belongings and keeping them sand-free. If you prefer, you can also bring personal items like a book or a beach chair for added comfort. Overall, focusing on comfort and convenience will help you make the most of your experience at the nude beach!

 **Law of the Land Hypothetical**

HYPOTHETICAL: *A group of friends decide to celebrate a birthday at a remote beach known for its relaxed nudist atmosphere. As the day goes on, one friend, feeling emboldened, starts dancing provocatively in a public area while nude, far from the designated nudist section. A passerby complains to the local authorities, who arrive and inform the group that public indecency laws apply, and that the friend's behavior could lead to arrest. What should the group do?*

ANSWER: *The group should act quickly and calmly. They can encourage their friend to stop the behavior immediately and cover up, acknowledging the seriousness of the situation. It's important for the group to remain respectful towards the authorities, as escalating tensions could worsen the situation and end up in an arrest and a criminal charge for immorality.*

UNUSUAL LAWS

- Overview
- Penalties and Fines
- General Questions
- Law of the Land Hypothetical

UNUSUAL LAWS

Overview

Unusual laws can provide fascinating glimpses into a culture's values and history. While most people are aware of common legal restrictions, it's often the strange and quirky laws that capture our attention. These regulations can range from the amusing to the absurd, reflecting the unique circumstances and traditions of a place. Whether they arise from historical events, societal norms, or simply peculiar local customs, unusual laws can provide insight into the quirks of human behavior and governance.

Here are a few of such unique Mexican laws:

- It's illegal to urinate in public, and authorities actively enforce this, especially against tourists who might think they can avoid detection.

- Drinking alcohol is prohibited for 72 hours before any state or national election, regardless of your citizenship status.

- Cyclists are not allowed to remove their feet from the pedals while riding. This law, established in the late 19th century, aims to prevent accidents.

- Bringing pork scratchings (and other pork products) from Mexico into the U.S. is illegal. Attempting to do so can result in arrest.

Penalties and Fines

Here's a look at the potential penalties for the unusual laws mentioned:

- **Public Urination:** Offenders can face fines or even arrest. The severity often depends on the location and circumstances, with authorities taking a stricter stance on tourists.

- **Drinking Before Elections:** Violating the alcohol ban during the 72 hours leading up to an election can result in fines or other legal repercussions, though enforcement may vary.

- **Cycling Feet Rule:** While not commonly enforced today, technically, violating this law could lead to fines or warnings, especially if it results in an accident.

- **Transporting Pork Products:** Attempting to bring pork scratchings into the U.S. can lead to confiscation of the items and potential fines or arrest, depending on the circumstances.

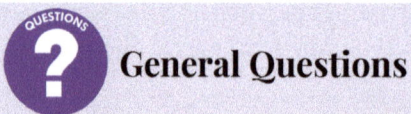 **General Questions**

1. *Is it illegal to wear camouflage clothing in Mexico?* **Yes**, wearing military-style camouflage clothing is illegal in Mexico, as it can be mistaken for military personnel. Violating this law can lead to fines or even detention.

2. *What happens if I fail to pay a fine in Mexico?* If you fail to pay a fine in Mexico, you may face additional penalties, such as increased fines, legal action, or even detention in more serious cases. It's best to address any fines promptly to avoid complications.

3. *Are there any laws about taking photos in Mexico?* **Yes**, in some areas, especially near military or police installations, taking photos is prohibited. Violating this can lead to confiscation of your camera or fines, so it's important to be aware of your surroundings.

 **Law of the Land Hypothetical**

HYPOTHETICAL: *On her last day of visiting Mexico City, Emily decides to buy some unique snacks to take home. She picks up a bag of pork cracklings from a store, thrilled to share them with family back home. What happens at the border when she tries to leave with the pork cracklings?*

ANSWER: *At the airport, customs officials tell Emily that bringing pork products into the U.S. is illegal. They confiscate the snacks and explain the potential fines for such violations.*

CHAPTER 21

TRAVELING SAFELY

CHAPTER 21

TRAVELING SAFELY

Ladies Traveling Solo

When people think of Mexico they often associate the country with te-quila, tacos, and colorful men with impressive mustaches, wearing sombreros and playing the guitar. A breathtaking place with dreamy sandy beaches, clear blue water, peppered with historical sites, but also a mysterious world of cartels, drugs and sex trafficking...a dangerous and scary country to travel to—especially if you are a woman! So, is traveling alone to Mexico safe?

In short, YES...with some caveats. Safety is subjective and cannot be absolutely guaranteed anywhere. It's essential to stay aware of your surroundings no matter where you find yourself and trust your instincts!

As with any visitor, when traveling alone as a woman in Mexico, it's important to steer clear of high-crime areas, particularly in states like Baja California, Chiapas, Chihuahua, and Guanajuato, as well as certain border towns and remote rural regions where the risk of kidnapping and violence is higher. Be a well-informed traveler: while some parts of the country have a "bad" reputation, many travelers visit them without issues. The reverse, of course, is also true: just because tourist areas are considered safe, some parts should still be avoided. The best practice is to always check current travel advisories and research your intended destination.

Here are some important safety precautions to take as a female solo traveler in Mexico:

- **Research your destination thoroughly:** Check current travel advisories and local news before visiting any area. Talk to the hotel or resort personnel or a trusted local what areas to avoid.
- **Stick to well-populated areas:** Avoid venturing into isolated areas, especially at night.
- **Use licensed taxis and ride-sharing services:** Be cautious about using street taxis and always confirm the route with the driver.
- **Inform someone of your plans:** Let a trusted friend or family member know your itinerary and expected return times.
- **Be aware of your surroundings:** Stay vigilant and trust your instincts.
- **Dress modestly in certain areas:** Depending on the region, dressing conservatively can help you avoid unwanted attention.
- **Learn basic Spanish phrases:** Knowing a few basic Spanish phrases can be helpful for communication.

 You can read about more personal experiences of some solo female travelers touring Mexico at:

- https://lisahomsy.com/solo-female-travel-mexico-travel-guide
- https://www.worldpackers.com/articles/solo-trip-to-mexico
- https://www.nomadicmatt.com/travel-blogs/solo-female-travel-mexico-safety/

Traveling as a Family

When traveling to Mexico with your family, it's important to prioritize safety by following some key tips. First, choose safe locations by sticking to well-known tourist areas such as Cancun, Riviera Maya, Merida, and San Miguel de Allende, which generally offer higher safety standards. Select reputable accommodations that have good security measures in place, like 24-hour front desks, surveillance cameras, and in-room safes.

Traveling in groups is highly advisable; avoid wandering alone, especially at night, and stay close to your family while exploring. Keep valuables secure by limiting the amount of cash you carry and storing important documents and valuables in your hotel safe. Use licensed transportation, opting only for registered taxis or reputable services.

Be fully aware of your surroundings by staying alert and exercising caution in unfamiliar areas. Avoid flashy displays by dressing modestly and refraining from wearing expensive jewelry to prevent attracting unwanted attention. It's also important to stay informed by checking local news and travel advisories before your trip and consider registering with your country's Smart Traveler Enrollment Program. (https://travel.state.gov/content/travel/en/international-travel/before-you-go/step.html)

Make sure to share your itinerary with family and friends back home, including details about your accommodation and contact information. Familiarize yourself with emergency contact information and carry a small first aid kit and any medications for your family. Have a conversation with your children about safety tips such as sticking together, not wandering off, and not talking to strangers. Always designate a meeting up point in case somebody gets lost.

Try to educate yourself about local customs and etiquette to prevent any cultural misunderstandings. Lastly, be mindful of alcohol consumption, especially in unfamiliar places, and always watch your drink. By following these guidelines, families can enhance their safety and enjoy a more secure travel experience in Mexico.

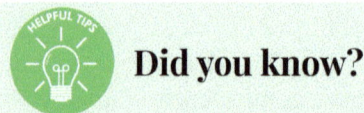

Did you know?

Children under 18 can enter Mexico on a parent's passport, but if not traveling with both parents, written consent from the absent parent is necessary.

For more advice on traveling in Mexico with kids, refer to https://www.roughguides.com/articles/mexico-with-kids.

Advice for All Travelers

Safety

Avoid protests and large public gatherings, which can become violent. Don't travel at night outside of major cities. Be aware of your surroundings, especially in crowded places.

Crime

Avoid buying, using, or being around drugs. Don't bring, sell, or purchase illicit substances; it is illegal and you could find yourself in a lot of trouble.

Driving

Use toll roads when possible and avoid driving alone or at night.

Health

Don't drink the tap water! Only drink from sealed water bottles. Avoid unpasteurized dairy products, raw or undercooked meat or fish, leafy greens, or raw vegetables. It's also best not to ask for ice in your drinks.

Money

Don't draw attention to your money or business affairs. Only use ATMs in public spaces and during the daytime. Split up your money and valuables.

Behavior

Don't push the boundaries of legality or behave in ways that you wouldn't in your country. Carrying weapons, vandalism, public urination, and public intoxication are not permitted.

Food

Stick to fruit that can be peeled, such as bananas and mangoes. Also avoid undercooked and uncooked foods as you are more prone to get sick.

Do's and Don'ts While in Mexico

Do's:

- **Engage with locals:** Try to learn a few basic Spanish phrases and use them when interacting with locals.
- **Try street food:** Sample the local cuisine but ensure it's from a reputable vendor.
- **Bargain at markets:** In some markets, it's acceptable to negotiate prices.
- **Visit cultural sites:** Explore historical landmarks like Mayan ruins and colonial towns.

Don'ts:

- **Don't be overly aggressive:** Avoid being pushy or demanding when interacting with locals.

- **Don't flaunt valuables:** Keep your valuables secure and avoid displaying large amounts of cash and expensive jewelry.

- **Don't drink and drive:** Always use designated drivers or taxis if consuming alcohol.

- **Don't take photos without permission:** Always ask before taking photos of people, especially in indigenous communities.

- **Don't rely solely on English:** While many people may speak English or at least understand it, try to learn basic Spanish phrases to show respect for Mexican culture.

Interaction with Locals

When interacting with locals in Mexico, it's important to approach the experience with respect and curiosity. Attending local events, such as religious ceremonies and festivals, allows you to engage with the culture authentically. Dining at smaller, authentic restaurants is a great way to savor regional cuisine and connect with the community.

Show genuine interest by asking questions and seeking clarification if something isn't clear. Locals often appreciate learning about you, so consider bringing photos or postcards from home to spark conversations. Always demonstrate respect, particularly toward older individuals, by yielding to them in public and allowing them to be served first. Handing objects directly to people rather than tossing them shows courtesy.

To avoid attracting unwanted attention, leave flashy jewelry, expensive watches, and overly provocative clothes at home. Be mindful of body language as well; certain gestures, like the "okay" sign, can be considered offensive, and putting your hands in your pockets or on your hips may come off as disrespectful or aggressive.

Finally, good conversation topics include discussing your impressions of Mexico, local football (soccer), and sharing details about your family and hobbies. By following these guidelines, you can foster positive interactions and deepen your cultural experience while in Mexico.

TOURIST TAXATION

CHAPTER 22
TOURIST TAXATION

Tourism Tax

The tourism tax in Mexico is a fee imposed by some states and municipalities to help fund local tourism infrastructure and services. Officially known as *Derecho No Residente* (DNR), this tax is included in the airfare and is required for visitors staying longer than seven days, in the amount of 687 pesos ($34.14 USD.)

Departure Tax

A departure tax in Mexico is a fee that travelers may have to pay when leaving the country, either by air or land. This tax is included in your airfare for all international departures from Mexico. Like the DNR, it requires no additional payment at the airport and will be listed on your airline receipt with a code of "TUA" or "XD." The amount is approximately $36 USD.

Certain individuals are exempt from the departure tax, including:[69]

- infants under two years old
- diplomats (excluding U.S. Embassy staff in Mexico)

---

69 https://www.aa.com/i18n/travel-info/international-travel/tax-exemptions.jsp

- deportees
- transit or transfer passengers who remain in Mexico for less than 24 hours

Additionally, the state of Quintana Roo imposes a mandatory visitor tax called VISITAX, applicable to all foreign tourists over 15 years old, regardless of how they exit the state. This tax is around $20 USD per person (with potential future increases) and can be paid at airport kiosks or online through the Visitax website. Failure to pay this tax may result in "observations" being noted on a visitor's passport for future trips to Quintana Roo.[70]

Guest Accommodation Tax

The lodging and vacation rental industry in Mexico is subject to two main taxes: VAT (Value Added Tax) and Lodging Tax.

VAT (Value Added Tax)

VAT in Mexico is set at 16% of the price charged, and all businesses must collect it, regardless of the owner's tax residency. If you have a property in Mexico, you must collect VAT from guests.

Lodging Tax

The lodging tax applies to listing prices in certain states, including Quintana Roo and Jalisco, with rates ranging from 2% to 7%. Like VAT, this tax is an additional charge.

Both VAT and the lodging tax are automatically included in all Airbnb listing prices, ensuring compliance. [71]

---

70 https://www.cancunairport.com/visitax.html

71 https://travelyucatan.com/mexico-travel-information/

Environmental/Sanitation Tax

This tax is determined by the municipality and collected by hotels or resorts, either at check-in or check-out. The rate varies between 20 to 70 pesos per night per room, which is approximately between $1 and $4 USD.

 **Law of the Land Hypothetical**

HYPOTHETICAL: *Sarah is planning a week-long vacation in Cancun, Mexico. She books an Airbnb for $300 per night and has some questions about the taxes she will encounter during her trip. What taxes will Sarah be responsible for when she books her Airbnb? How much will she actually pay per night? Are there any other taxes or fees that Sarah should be aware of?*

ANSWER: *Sarah will need to pay VAT (16%) which Airbnb will automatically add to her booking and the Lodging Tax which varies by municipality, typically ranging from 2% to 7%.*

For a nightly rate of $300, the VAT would be $48 and Lodging Tax approximately $21 (7%). Therefore, Sarah's total per night would be around $369, assuming the lodging tax is based on the nightly rate.

In addition to the VAT and Lodging Tax, Sarah should be aware of the Visitax, a tourist tax for visitors to Quintana Roo. This tax is approximately $20 and can be paid online before or during her visit. While it's not strictly enforced, it's a good idea to pay it to comply with local regulations.

LONG-TERM STAYS

LONG-TERM STAYS

Overview

People choose to stay long-term in Mexico for various reasons. One significant factor is the cost of living, which is generally lower than in many countries, including the U.S., covering expenses like food, utilities, and homeownership. The warm climate is another appealing aspect, providing pleasant weather year-round.

Mexico is also famous for its delicious cuisine, with access to fresh, wholesome food at affordable prices. Healthcare is more affordable too, encompassing routine medical care, specialist services, and medications.

Culturally, Mexico is known for its laid-back atmosphere and friendly people, often described as a collectivist society where individuals look out for one another. Additionally, many people report positive lifestyle changes, such as healthier eating habits, increased physical activity, more socializing, and a slower pace of life.

Visa and Residency Requirements

For those looking to stay longer, there are a few options:

- **Temporary Resident Visa:** This visa is for foreign nationals and their families who want to settle in Mexico. It can be issued for a year and renewed annually for up to three years. To apply, you must prove you meet certain requirements, such as having a minimum bank balance or monthly income.

- **Permanent Resident Visa:** This visa is for people who want to live in Mexico indefinitely. You can apply for a Permanent Resident Visa if you meet certain requirements, such as:

  - Having close family ties to a Mexican citizen or permanent resident

  - Applying for retirement status and proving you have enough monthly income or savings

  - Having four years of regular Temporary Resident status

  - Being granted residency on humanitarian grounds or through political asylum

  - You can apply for a Permanent Resident Visa at a Mexican consulate outside of Mexico.[72]

Healthcare Options

Foreigners can access healthcare in Mexico if they hold a valid temporary or permanent residence visa. However, those on a standard tourist visa cannot work or enroll in the national healthcare system. If employed by a Mexican company, expats are automatically enrolled in the national healthcare scheme. Retirees or self-employed individuals must enroll voluntarily and pay a fee.

For short-term stays, visitors with a working tourist visa can work for up to 180 days and may be covered by corporate travel insurance, which should include comprehensive benefits. Long-term expats qualify for national healthcare under Mexico's social security scheme, which requires contributions from both employers and employees for coverage of emergencies and medications. Many opt for supplemental insurance for quicker access to care.

---

72 https://www.mexperience.com/lifestyle/living-in-mexico/
    visas-and-immigration/

Expats can choose public health insurance through the Instituto Mexicano del Seguro Social (IMSS) or private health insurance. IMSS covers basic medical needs but excludes dental and elective services. Enrollment is automatic for employed residents and requires documentation for voluntary participants.

Employers often provide supplemental private insurance to ensure access to higher-quality care.[73]

Long-Term Housing Options

Expats moving to Mexico have various accommodation options, with urban housing generally more expensive than in rural areas. Options include colonial-style detached houses, modern apartments and condos—especially beachfront properties, which can be pricey—shared flats for young professionals, and larger countryside homes with extensive gardens.

When deciding whether to rent furnished or unfurnished, furnished accommodations often require no extra deposit and are preferred by those staying short-term. Short-term rental agreements are advisable for newcomers to allow time for neighborhood exploration.

Rental contracts in Mexico typically include short-term, six-month, and long-term agreements. Rental costs are generally lower than in many countries, influenced by factors such as location, property size, and amenities. Major cities like Mexico City, Los Cabos, and Cancun have higher rents, while places like Tlaxcala and Tepic offer more affordable options.

To rent, start by researching housing platforms like Airbnb for short stays or Vivanuncios (https://www.vivanuncios.com.mx/) for long-term rentals. Real estate agencies can also assist, with their fees often covered by landlords. Once you find a place, review the rental contract with a lawyer, as landlords may require a co-signer or guarantor, typically a Mexican citizen. You'll need to pay the first month's rent plus a deposit,

---

73 https://www.internationalinsurance.com/health/north-america/mexico.
php)

ideally via bank transfer for record-keeping. Common required documents include proof of identity, residency, and employment. Some landlords may also request credit checks, banking information, or reference letters from previous landlords.[74]

Getting Around

Living in Mexico offers great travel opportunities, as the country has diverse destinations and ample transportation options. While it may seem small on a map, Mexico's size and variety can be surprising. Travel can be done by plane, bus, car, or taxi, depending on your schedule and destination.

Air travel is convenient, with around 50 airports, including major hubs in Mexico City and Cancun. National airlines like Aeromexico and Volaris often provide affordable domestic flights, making air travel quicker and sometimes cheaper than long-distance bus trips. Keep in mind that airport fees (TUA) are increasing annually.

Buses are the most common mode of transport, with extensive networks in cities and towns. First-class buses offer comfort, while second-class buses are more affordable but still pleasant. Local buses and colectivos (vans) serve urban areas and are inexpensive but can be noisy.

Taxis in Mexico often lack meters, so it's best to confirm the fare upfront. Using hotel-recommended taxis or rideshare services like Uber is safer than hailing cabs on the street. Be cautious if using street taxis, checking for identification and vehicle condition.

Mexico City has an efficient subway system, which can be quicker than buses during rush hour. Tickets are inexpensive, and there are also other bus services like Metrobus and Trolebus. For road trips, renting a car provides flexibility, but drivers need Mexican insurance and may face hidden costs.

---

74   https://www.pacificprime.lat/blog/
     expats-guide-to-renting-a-house-in-mexico/

Best Places for Expats to Live in Mexico

With well over a million expats, Mexico is the top destination for North Americans moving abroad. The best place to relocate within Mexico depends on personal preferences. Some may prefer off-grid living or small villages with minimal foreign presence, while others might opt for areas where they can avoid local interactions and language barriers. Most expats seek a balance, looking for locations that offer an easy transition, good amenities, and vibrant local culture. Here are a few expat-friendly communities fitting this middle ground:[75]

1. **Puerto Vallarta** has been an expat haven for over 60 years, transforming from a small village into a major resort destination along Banderas Bay. The surrounding Riviera Nayarit offers diverse activities, from exploring the malecón and enjoying golf to hiking in the Sierra Madre mountains and engaging in water sports.

2. **San Miguel de Allende** is a picturesque colonial town with a vibrant arts scene and a sizable expat community, allowing for both English and Spanish communication. While lacking an international airport, it is accessible via nearby León or Querétaro.

3. **Mérida**, a larger colonial city in the Yucatán, boasts a rich cultural scene and safety, along with an international airport. It offers opportunities to learn Spanish and enjoy the unique Yucatán cuisine.

4. **Lake Chapala** is home to the largest concentration of U.S. expats, featuring a pleasant climate and affordable living. The area is known for its artistic community and active lifestyle options.

5. **Tulum**, on the Riviera Maya, combines a bohemian vibe with modern development and stunning Caribbean beaches, making it a popular expat destination.

6. **Huatulco**, a planned tourist development, is emerging as a destination with a small population, excellent amenities, and a focus on outdoor activities.

---

75 https://internationalliving.com/best-places-live-mexico-u-s-expat/

7. **Los Cabos**, located at the southern tip of the Baja California peninsula, is renowned for its beaches, modern conveniences, and vibrant nightlife, making it a favorite among expats and tourists alike.

Local Community Integration

Expats looking to integrate into local communities in Mexico can take several steps. One of the most valuable is learning Spanish, which opens up opportunities to connect with locals and immerse oneself in Mexican culture. Cities like Mexico City offer various language-exchange events organized by schools, cultural centers, and expat meetups, making it easier to practice.

Joining expat groups is another great way to establish connections. Social media platforms like Facebook and Meetup host numerous groups where expats can share experiences, ask questions, and participate in events. In Mexico City, groups such as InterNations and Foreigners & Expats in Mexico City are popular choices. Additionally, InterNations offers specialized groups for activities like sightseeing and hiking, fostering a sense of community among members. Visiting established expat communities in coastal cities like Puerto Vallarta, Huatulco, and Mérida can also provide a welcoming environment for newcomers.

Overall, Mexico has consistently ranked high in the Expat Insider "Survey's Ease of Settling In Index," reflecting the friendliness of local residents and the ease with which expats can forge friendships.

 For more information on how to join an expat community in Mexico, visit **https://www.internations.org/mexico-expats/americans.**

 **General Questions Stays**

1. ***If I want to stay in Mexico long-term and work, should I apply for a work permit before arriving in Mexico?*** **Yes**. To work in Mexico long-term, you need to apply for a temporary resident visa with work authorization before you arrive, as working on a tourist visa is not permitted. This process requires securing a job offer from a Mexican employer, who will sponsor your visa application. You must submit your application through the Mexican consulate in your home country, where you'll provide the necessary paperwork. Once you arrive in Mexico, you are required to register with the immigration authorities within a specified period to complete the process.

   For more information, please refer to https://www.globalization-partners.com/globalpedia/mexico/visa-permits/.

2. ***I am American. Can I retire to Mexico?*** **Yes**. Mexico is a popular retirement destination for Americans, offering a lower cost of living and warmer weather. A couple can live comfortably on about $2,500 per month, depending on your lifestyle, though costs vary by location. To retire in Mexico long-term, you need a resident visa, with income requirements such as a pension or investments that meet the Mexican government's criteria.

   Housing is affordable, with rentals starting at $400 USD a month and homes to purchase starting at $200,000 USD. Healthcare is high-quality and much cheaper than in the U.S.

   U.S. retirees can receive Social Security payments in Mexico but must continue filing taxes. Mexico offers diverse lifestyles, from city living to rural tranquility, making it a great choice for retirees seeking an affordable, fulfilling life.

 **Law of the Land Hypothetical**

HYPOTHETICAL: *Sarah, a 58-year-old retiree from the U.S., loves the idea of retiring in Mexico. After visiting several times, she's decided on Lake Chapala, drawn by its expat community, warm climate, and affordable living. She's now looking into the visa process for a long-term stay. Can Sarah stay in Mexico long-term as a retiree, and what steps does she need to take?*

ANSWER: *Yes, Sarah can stay long-term by applying for a permanent resident visa. She'll need to prove monthly income of at least $2,700 (from pensions or investments) and submit her application at a Mexican consulate in the U.S. After approval, she can live in Mexico indefinitely. Sarah can also continue receiving U.S. Social Security while living in Mexico but must file U.S. taxes on her global income. Consulting with a financial advisor will help her manage retirement funds and taxes while adjusting to life in Mexico.*

 **Takeaways**

- **Visas:** To stay long-term, apply for a temporary or permanent resident visa—tourist visas don't allow for extended stays or work.

- **Income Requirements:** You'll need to prove financial stability through income, savings, or pension for visa approval.

- **Healthcare:** Mexico's healthcare is affordable and good quality, with options like private insurance or IMSS (Mexico's social security).

- **Cost of Living:** A comfortable life can cost around $2,500/month for a couple, depending on location and lifestyle.

- **Residency Process:** Apply for visas through a Mexican consulate in your home country, then register with immigration upon arrival.

- **Taxes:** U.S. citizens are taxed on global income, so you'll need to comply with both U.S. and Mexican tax laws.

- **Expat Communities:** Popular expat hubs include Puerto Vallarta, Lake Chapala, and San Miguel de Allende. Mexico is known for its friendly locals and ease of integration.

- **Housing:** Rent can start at $400/month, and buying property is possible through a bank trust for foreigners.

- **Overstay Consequences:** Overstaying a visa can result in fines or deportation, so it's important to keep track of your status.

CHAPTER 24

CIVIL LITIGATION

IN THIS CHAPTER

- Overview
- Personal Injury Claims and Compensation Law
- How to File a Civil Claim
- Service of Documents
- Statute of Limitations
- Getting Married in Mexico

CIVIL LITIGATION

Overview

Civil litigation provides a mechanism for resolving disputes, ensuring that travelers have a way to seek justice if legal issues arise while visiting another country. It helps them understand their rights and obligations under local laws, which may differ from those in their home country. The civil litigation system offers a formal process for addressing conflicts, such as contract disputes or personal injury claims, and can deter unfair practices by encouraging businesses to comply with legal standards. It also allows individuals to seek financial recourse for damages or losses and helps protect them from potential exploitation by local entities. Overall, understanding civil litigation enhances a visitor's experience and safety while traveling.

Personal Injury Claims and Compensation Law

If you suffer a physical, emotional, or financial injury while in Mexico, you may have grounds for a personal injury case. Personal injury refers to harm caused to your body by another's actions. In tourist areas like resorts, the Tourism Law mandates that service providers ensure guest safety through appropriate security measures.

You may have a valid claim if:[76]

- The accident wasn't your fault.
- Negligence by another party (like a driver or property owner) caused your injury (e.g., slip-and-fall accidents due to wet floors, poor maintenance, or inadequate lighting).
- You required medical attention.
- You lost wages or incurred medical expenses.

Personal injury cases can involve various types of injuries resulting from another party's negligence, including slip and falls, accidents during tourism activities, car accidents, food poisoning, assault, medical malpractice, or wrongful death.

 **It's important to consult with a Mexican lawyer to assess your situation.**

Personal injury lawyers typically request a small retainer at the beginning, with the balance of their fees being deducted from any settlement once the case is resolved. In most cases, personal injury claims are settled outside of court, with the lawyer negotiating fair compensation for medical expenses and lost wages. If necessary, your lawyer will decide whether to take the case to trial, and in most instances, your lawyer can represent you without your physical appearance in court.

To support your case, seek medical attention right away, contact a personal injury lawyer, and gather evidence such as photos of the location where the injury occurred (e.g., wet floors, uneven surfaces, or obstacles). In the case of a vehicle accident, collect details like the other driver's ID, insurance information, witness contact info, and a police report. Always review any paperwork with your lawyer before signing and keep all receipts and invoices related to medical expenses or other costs incurred due to the injury.

---

76 https://mexlaw.com/determining-a-personal-injury-case-in-mexico/

Statute of Limitations

The statute of limitations for personal injury cases in Mexico is determined by the state in which the accident occurred, not by your citizenship. Typically, it is two years, but it can vary by state. The statute of limitations starts from the date of the injury, and it's important to account for all potential long-term effects of the injury before deciding to pursue a claim. Delays in filing or pursuing the case can complicate dealings with insurance companies, so it's crucial to seek legal help promptly.

Most personal injury cases are resolved through settlement with insurance companies rather than through litigation. However, an extrajudicial claim (e.g., settlement negotiations) does not pause the statute of limitations, so it's important to begin the settlement process early.

Documentation

Key documentation for your claim includes:

- Accident reports
- Medical records and bills
- Witness contact information
- Photos of injuries and damaged property
- Insurance details
- Police reports (if applicable)

When filing a claim, the first step is determining if the person or business responsible has insurance. If so, you can file a third-party claim with their insurer. Insurance companies often offer settlements to avoid expensive and lengthy litigation.

If you're in Mexico and need assistance, the U.S. Embassy can help you find medical care or a doctor. For legal help with a personal injury case in Mexico, you can consult with an experienced Mexican attorney.

Damages

In Mexico, damages for personal injury cases are calculated based on the actual harm caused to the victim, which includes both economic and non-economic losses. The primary factors taken into account are:

- Medical Expenses
- Loss of Income
- Pain and Suffering
- Permanent Disability or Disfigurement
- Property Damage
- Legal Costs
- Punitive Damages (in rare cases)

In many cases, personal injury claims in Mexico are settled out of court, and the final compensation amount is negotiated between the injured party and the defendant or their insurance company. If the case goes to trial, a judge will determine the damages based on the evidence presented.

The final amount of compensation can vary greatly depending on the nature of the injury, the extent of damages, and the local laws in the state where the incident occurred.

How to File a Civil Claim

Filing a civil claim in Mexico can be complex, especially if you're not familiar with the local legal system. For this reason, it's highly recommended to work with an attorney who specializes in Mexican law to guide you through the process and ensure your claim is properly filed.

In civil claims in Mexico, the judge serves as both the finder of facts and the interpreter of the law. While the judge may order the gathering of evidence, this is uncommon, and the parties are generally responsible for preparing and submitting their own evidence. The parties have limited control over the procedural rules and timelines, although in commercial matters, they may agree on certain aspects of the process.

To file a civil claim in Mexico, the process begins with preparing the claim, ensuring that any doubts are clarified and preliminary obstacles removed. The lawsuit is then filed with the court, which will either admit, dismiss, or request clarification on the case. If the lawsuit is admitted, the defendant is given a set period to respond. Both parties will then exchange written arguments and evidence. A preliminary hearing is scheduled by the judge, during which the parties can discuss the case and potentially reach an agreement. Afterward, closing arguments are submitted in writing, and the judge will make a decision on the case.

 **Note: there are no jury trials in civil cases in Mexico! In fact, Mexico does not have jury trials in any cases, except for treason.**[77]

Where to file?

To file a civil claim in Mexico, you must determine the correct court, based on the location of the defendant or the incident.

- **State Civil Courts:** For most general civil cases (e.g., personal injury, contracts), file in the state court where the defendant lives or the event occurred.
- **Mexico City (CDMX):** File in the civil courts within Mexico City if the case involves this region.
- **Federal Courts:** If the claim involves federal law (e.g., taxes, constitutional rights), file in a federal court.
- **Specialized Courts:** For family law, commercial disputes, or labor cases, file in the appropriate specialized court.

---

[77] https://iclg.com/practice-areas/
litigation-and-dispute-resolution-laws-and-regulations/mexico

- **Local or Municipal Courts:** For minor claims with smaller amounts, file in local or municipal courts.
- **Online Filing:** Some states allow electronic filing for minor claims.

Service of Documents

Service of documents refers to the official delivery of legal documents to the parties involved in a case, ensuring that they are informed of the legal proceedings.

Process

In civil litigation in Mexico, service of process is typically carried out by an authorized court clerk known as an actuario. The clerk is responsible for delivering documents to the defendant at their residence or business. If the defendant or their legal representative is unavailable, the actuario can serve a relative, employee, or other household member after confirming the location is the defendant's domicile.

The service includes a writ detailing the date, time, type of proceedings, the parties involved, the court hearing the case, relevant court rulings, and the name of the person receiving the documents. Copies of the plaintiff's complaint and supporting documents are also attached. If the plaintiff is unsure of the defendant's address, the court may request information from authorities or companies. If the address cannot be found, the court can order service by publication in a newspaper.

In commercial litigation, Mexico's Federal Code of Commerce outlines similar procedures for the serving process. Since June 2020, parties in commercial cases may opt to receive notifications electronically. If they do not, the traditional process applies. Electronic notifications are effective when the recipient accesses the document through a court system, and confirmation is automatically recorded.[78]

---

78 https://maint.loc.gov/law/help/service-of-process/mexico.php

Proof of Service

In Mexico, proof of service is provided by the Acta de Notificación, an official certificate confirming that legal documents were properly delivered. This document includes details such as the date, method, and recipient of service. For international cases, the Ministry of Foreign Affairs issues the proof when using the Hague Service Convention. The Acta de Notificación serves as legal evidence that the recipient was notified according to the law.

Statute of Limitations

The statute of limitations in Mexico for civil suits varies depending on the type of claim. The general rules and specific timeframes are governed by the Civil Code of each state and the Federal Civil Code for federal matters.

 **Statute of Limitations for Different Types of Civil Claims**

- **General Civil Claims (eg. property disputes, breach of contract):** 10 years

- **Property and Real Estate Claims:** 5 years

- **Labor Disputes:** 1 year

- **Inheritance and Family Law Claims:** 5 years

The length of the statute of limitations in Mexico can be influenced by several factors. The type of claim directly determines the applicable time limits. Additionally, in cases where the harm or damage is not immediately apparent—such as with personal injury or fraud—the statute of limitations may start from the date the injury or damage was discovered, rather than when it occurred. If the claimant is a minor or incapacitated, the statute of limitations may be suspended until the individual reaches adulthood or regains capacity.

What Happens if a Civil Suit is Filed After the Statute of Limitations Has Expired?

In the event of statute of limitations expiring, there are two possible outcomes:

- **Dismissal:** If a civil suit is filed after the statute of limitations has expired, the defendant can request the court to dismiss the case. The court will likely reject the claim, as it's no longer considered valid or enforceable due to the time limit having passed.

- **Exceptions for Delayed Claims:** If the claimant can prove reasons for the delay (such as fraud, force majeure, or the defendant's actions preventing the claimant from filing), the court may consider the case on its merits.

Extending the Statute of Limitations

The statute of limitations in Mexico can be extended in certain situations. It may be suspended if the defendant is outside the country, the claimant is a minor, or the claimant is mentally incapacitated.

The statute can also be interrupted if the defendant acknowledges the claim, or if legal actions, such as settlement negotiations, occur. Additionally, if the defendant hides evidence of damage or fraud, the statute of limitations may be extended until the concealment is discovered.

Getting Married in Mexico

Legal Requirements

To get married in Mexico, certain legal requirements must be met. First, obtain a marriage permit from the Mexican consulate before arriving. When applying at the Civil Registry Office, you'll need to present certain documents: a completed application, valid passport, certified and apostilled birth certificate (translated into Spanish), and, if applicable, a divorce decree or death certificate from previous marriages. You'll also need four witnesses with valid IDs, and you must undergo health tests (blood test and chest X-ray) in Mexico within 14 days of the wedding.

Age Requirements

Both parties must be at least 18 years old to marry without parental consent. If under 18, a parent must be present.

Residency Requirements

There are no residency requirements for foreign nationals to marry in Mexico, but a passport and tourist visa are required, and additional paperwork may be necessary if marrying a Mexican citizen or resident.

Civil v. Religious Marriage

Mexico legally recognizes only civil marriages; you must register your marriage at the Civil Registry Office (Registro Civil). The ceremony will be performed by a government official and is usually brief. A religious ceremony (e.g., Catholic, Protestant) can be performed separately but does not have legal standing on its own. If you wish to have a religious ceremony, you will need to first complete the civil marriage process. Afterward, a religious ceremony can be conducted, but it does not substitute for the legal civil process.

Fees for Getting Married

The fees for a civil marriage in Mexico vary by location but typically range from $30 to $150 USD, depending on the state and the services provided. Additional costs might include document translation, apostille fees, and any administrative fees for health tests or other required paperwork.

Marriage Registration

After the civil ceremony, the marriage will be officially registered with the Civil Registry Office. You will receive a marriage certificate (acta de matrimonio), which is valid worldwide. To use this certificate outside of Mexico, you may need to get it legalized or apostilled by Mexican authorities to ensure it is recognized by foreign governments. This process is typically done at the Secretary of Foreign Affairs (SRE) in Mexico.[79]

---

79 https://embamex.sre.gob.mx/hungria/index.php/en/consular-services/
marriage-in-mexico

CHAPTER 25

OTHER THINGS TO KNOW

OTHER THINGS TO KNOW

Tourists and Street Hustling

Mexico is known for street hustling, particularly in tourist areas. It can vary by region, with some areas experiencing higher rates of incidents than others. In cities like Mexico City, Cancun, and Playa del Carmen, you'll encounter a range of street vendors, performers, and hustlers. While many street vendors offer legitimate products and services, the presence of aggressive sales tactics, money solicitation, and occasional scams can be notable.

Common forms of street hustling include persistent vendors who may follow tourists in an attempt to sell souvenirs or food, which can feel intrusive. Tourists might also encounter scams, such as fake tours or overpriced goods, and individuals posing as officials to solicit money. Street performers often seek tips, and while many are talented, some may pressure tourists for money after their performances.

Safety Concerns and Practical Tips

While street hustling can be frustrating, it often reflects the vibrant local economy. Staying informed and aware can help you navigate these situations more comfortably.

Safety concerns related to street hustling for tourists include aggressive behavior, where some hustlers use high-pressure tactics that can make people feel uncomfortable. Scams are common, with tourists potentially falling victim to misleading offers, fake products, or inflated prices. The crowded environments where hustling occurs also increase the risk of pickpocketing.

Unlicensed services pose additional risks, as those offering transportation or tours may not adhere to safety regulations. Misinformation can mislead tourists about local attractions, while health risks arise from food vendors who may not follow hygiene practices. Disputes between hustlers or with tourists can escalate, leading to physical confrontations. Overall, the constant pressure to engage can create emotional distress, detracting from tourists' enjoyment. Awareness of these issues can help visitors navigate street hustling more safely.

To navigate street hustling, it helps to be firm but polite when approached by a vendor or performer; a simple "no, thank you" usually suffices. Setting a budget can also be beneficial, allowing you to know how much you're willing to spend on souvenirs or experiences. Familiarizing yourself with common scams in the areas you'll visit can help you avoid falling victim. Engaging with caution is key—if you're interested in purchasing something, it's best to do so from established vendors or markets to ensure fair pricing.

Efforts are being made by local authorities and tourism boards to improve safety measures and enhance the overall visitor experience. Travelers are advised to stay informed, use reputable services, and take precautions to minimize risks.

Official public transportation vehicles have red license plates. Private vehicles, NOT licensed for public transportation, have white license plates with blue letters/numbers. Only use licensed taxicabs with red-and-white PP license plates or recommended transportation services. Do not accept rides from strangers.

 ## In the Event of Death

If you are visiting Mexico and experience a death of someone you know, the first crucial step is to contact the nearest U.S. embassy or consulate to report the death and receive assistance with navigating the local procedures for handling the deceased, including coordinating with a local funeral home and obtaining necessary documentation to transport the remains back to the U.S. if needed; they will also try to locate and inform the next of kin.

Key actions to take:

- **Notify authorities:** Immediately contact the local police or medical authorities to report the death.

- **Contact the embassy:** Reach out to the U.S. embassy or consulate in Mexico to inform them of the situation and request assistance.

- **Identify next of kin:** If possible, locate and contact the deceased person's next of kin to inform them about the death.

- **Funeral arrangements:** The embassy can help you find a local funeral home to manage the burial or cremation process.

- **Documentation:** Ensure you have all necessary documentation, including the deceased person's passport and any relevant medical records.

- **Consular Mortuary Certificate:** The embassy will issue a Consular Mortuary Certificate, which is required for transporting the remains internationally.

Important considerations:

- **Local laws and customs:** Be aware of Mexican laws regarding death and burial practices, which may differ from your home country.

- **Insurance coverage:** Check your travel insurance policy to understand what coverage is available for death abroad, including repatriation of remains.

- **Power of Attorney:** Consider having a legal power of attorney in place to allow a designated person to make decisions on your behalf in case you become incapacitated.[80, 81] Please note that death terminates a POA.

Experiencing Financial Hardship

If you are a U.S. citizen facing financial hardship while abroad, you should contact the nearest U.S. embassy or consulate or reach out to the U.S. Department of State's Office of Overseas Citizens Services at +1 202-501-4444. They can assist you in several ways. First, consular officers can help you arrange for funds to be transferred from family, your bank, or your employer. In certain situations, the Department of State can wire funds directly to you. Additionally, you may be eligible to apply for a repatriation loan, which the U.S. government might provide to help cover your return to the United States, including transportation, food, lodging, fees, and medical expenses.

You can also consider other options, such as using a commercial money transfer service like Western Union or MoneyGram to receive funds. If you have any valuable items, selling them could provide you with some quick cash.[82]

---

80 https://mx.usembassy.gov/death-of-a-u-s-citizen

81 https://travel.state.gov/content/travel/en/international-travel/while-abroad/death-abroad1.html

82 https://travel.state.gov/content/travel/en/international-travel/emergencies/emergency-financial-assistance.html

To stretch your budget, make a list of essential expenses and look for more affordable accommodations, such as hostels, and opt for meals at local markets instead of restaurants. If you have the right visa, consider temporary work opportunities, like teaching English or freelancing online. Contact your bank or credit card company, as they might assist you in accessing emergency funds or increasing your ATM withdrawal limits.

Be wary of scams and trust your instincts if something seems off. Once you've stabilized your situation, create a daily budget to help manage your expenses and consider using public transportation to save money. Lastly, document all financial transactions and communications to avoid confusion and ensure clarity in your dealings.

QUICK REFERENCE GUIDE

- Quick Chapter References to Important Topics

CHAPTER 26

QUICK REFERENCE GUIDE

Crime in Mexico

Are there particular areas I should avoid as a tourist?

Yes. While many parts of Mexico are safe for tourists, certain regions, particularly near the U.S. border (e.g., Tijuana, Ciudad Juárez) and states with high cartel activity (e.g., Sinaloa, Guerrero, Michoacán), can be risky due to organized crime and violence. Major tourist destinations like Cancun, Mexico City, Puerto Vallarta, and the Yucatán Peninsula (e.g., Mérida, Playa del Carmen) are generally considered safe but should still be navigated with caution, especially at night. *For more details, see Chapter 3.*

Drug Offenses

Is the possession of marijuana legal?

Possession of **up to 28 grams** of marijuana for personal use is decriminalized (legal) in Mexico, following a Supreme Court ruling in 2021. However, recreational sales and distribution remain illegal, and the government is still working on regulating the legal market.

Is the possession of cocaine legal?

No. Possession of cocaine is illegal in Mexico, and even small amounts can lead to criminal charges. Penalties vary, but trafficking or distribution carries severe legal consequences. *For more details, see Chapter 4.*

Alcohol-Related Offenses

What is the legal drinking age?

The legal drinking age in Mexico is **18**. This applies to both residents and tourists, and identification may be required when purchasing alcohol.

What is the legal blood alcohol limit?

The legal blood alcohol limit for driving in Mexico is generally **0.08%** for regular drivers, but some states have stricter limits or zero-tolerance policies, especially for commercial drivers. Driving under the influence can lead to fines, arrests, or worse. *For more details, see Chapter 5.*

Firearm & Ammunition Offenses

Can I possess a gun?

Yes. In Mexico, civilian gun ownership is highly restricted. However, you can possess a firearm only with a permit, which is difficult to obtain and requires justification (e.g., self-defense, sport shooting). Only certain types of guns are allowed, and they must be registered with the government.

Can I possess ammunition?

Depends. Possessing ammunition without a license is illegal in Mexico. Ammunition can only be owned if you have a legal firearm permit for the specific type of ammo, and unauthorized possession of ammunition can lead to serious legal consequences. *For more details, see Chapter 6.*

Prostitution

Is prostitution legal?

Yes, prostitution is legal in Mexico, but it is regulated. It is allowed in designated areas or "tolerance zones" in some cities, where sex work is controlled for health and safety. However, pimping, trafficking, and exploitation are illegal. *For more details, see Chapter 7.*

LGBTQ

Is homosexuality legal?

Yes, homosexuality is legal in Mexico. Same-sex relationships have been decriminalized, and LGBTQ+ rights are protected under Mexican law.

Are same sex public displays of affection legal?

Yes, same-sex public displays of affection are legal in Mexico. However, societal acceptance can vary by region, with more liberal attitudes in larger cities like Mexico City and less tolerance in rural areas. *For more details, see Chapter 8.*

Arrested in Mexico

Would I be entitled to bail if I'm arrested?

Typically, **yes**. You may be entitled to bail, depending on the nature of the crime and whether it's considered a serious offense. Bail is typically allowed for non-violent crimes, but it can be denied for more severe charges.

Will a lawyer be provided to me if I cannot afford one?

Yes, if you cannot afford a lawyer, you are entitled to legal representation through a public defender under Mexican law. You should request one immediately after being detained. *For more details, see Chapter 10.*

Helping a Friend or Relative Imprisoned in Mexico

Can I send money to a friend or relative imprisoned in Mexico?

Yes, you can send money to a friend or family member in prison, but it must go through official channels like the prison's authorized banking system or other approved methods.

Can I remain in Mexico upon release from prison or jail after my sentence is complete?

Yes, you can remain in Mexico after completing your sentence, but you may need to ensure your visa or legal status is in order if you were arrested while in the country. *For more details, see Chapter 12.*

Crime Victim Assistance

Can a victim of a crime be legally compensated?

Yes, victims of crime in Mexico can seek compensation through civil lawsuits or restitution as part of the legal process, though this depends on the circumstances of the case.

Does the Mexican government offer assistance for family members of homicide victims?

Yes, the Mexican government provides assistance to family members of homicide victims, including financial aid, psychological support, and legal guidance through various government programs. *For more details, see Chapter 14.*

Police

Is there an official police force?

Yes, Mexico has an official police force, which includes multiple agencies such as the Federal Police, State Police, and Municipal Police, each is responsible for different levels of law enforcement. *For more details, see Chapter 15.*

How to Get Legal Help in Mexico

Is there a resource in Mexico to find legal representation?

Yes, you can find legal representation in Mexico through local bar associations, law firms, or online directories like the Mexican Bar Association (Barra Mexicana).

Is there free legal representation assistance?

Yes, Mexico offers free legal assistance for those who cannot afford a lawyer through public defenders provided by the government, particularly for criminal cases. *For more details, see Chapter 16.*

Foreign Embassies in Mexico

Are there foreign embassies in Mexico?

Yes, Mexico hosts foreign embassies from various countries, primarily located in Mexico City.

Is there a website to locate embassies in Mexico?

Yes, you can locate embassies in Mexico through the Ministry of Foreign Affairs website or by visiting the embassy's official website directly. *For more details, see Chapter 16.*

Medical Facilities & Hospitals

Is there a number I can call for ambulance and fire emergencies?

Yes, in Mexico, you can call **911** for ambulance, fire, and police emergencies.

If I am injured while on vacation in Mexico, are there hospitals that are recommended for tourists?

Yes, many tourist destinations have hospitals with English-speaking staff and facilities for international visitors. Some recommended hospitals include Hospital Angeles and Hospital Médica Sur in Mexico City, Hospiten in Cancun, and Amerimed in Playa del Carmen. *For more details, see Chapter 17.*

Driving in Mexico

Which side of the road do I drive on?

In Mexico, you drive on the **right side** of the road.

Can I use my driver's license from my home country to drive in Mexico?

Yes, you can use your foreign driver's license to drive in Mexico as a tourist, typically for up to 180 days.

How old do I need to be to rent a car?

The minimum age to rent a car in Mexico is generally **21**, although some rental agencies may require drivers to be at least 25 or charge an additional fee for drivers under 25. *For more details, see Chapter 18.*

Nude Beaches & Clothing-Optional Resorts

Is public nudity legal on all beaches in Mexico?

No. Public nudity is generally illegal in Mexico. However, there are designated clothing-optional resorts and beaches, where nudity is allowed in specific zones. Always check local regulations before visiting. *For more details, see Chapter 19.*

Tourist Taxation

Is there a room tax in Mexico?

Yes, in Mexico, there is often a room tax or hospitality tax applied to hotel stays. This tax varies by location and is typically added to your bill at checkout. *For more details, see Chapter 22.*

Is there any fee associated with leaving Mexico?

Yes, there is a tourist tax (often called a departure tax) for international travelers leaving Mexico, which is typically included in the cost of your airline ticket. However, in some cases, you may need to pay it separately at the airport. *For more details, see Chapter 22.*

Long-Term Stays

Do I need to return to my home country to apply for a work permit in Mexico?

Yes. Generally, if you're applying for a work permit in Mexico, you need to do so through a Mexican consulate in your home country or country of residence. However, some processes may be completed within Mexico under certain conditions.

As an American, how long can I stay in Mexico without a visa?

As an American, you can stay in Mexico for up to **180 days** (about six months) as a tourist without a visa. This is typically granted upon entry, but you must show proof of return travel and sufficient funds. *For more details, see Chapter 23.*

In the Event of Death

What documents would an embassy need regarding the death of a tourist?

If a tourist dies in Mexico, the embassy will need the death certificate, the deceased's passport or ID, medical records, proof of next of kin, and travel insurance details if available. The embassy will assist with repatriation and legal matters. *For more details, see Chapter 25.*

U.S. Consulate Assistance

Are there any limitations to the consulate assistance I can receive while in Mexico?

Yes. Consulates in Mexico can assist with passport issues, emergency repatriation, and legal documents, but they cannot provide legal representation, financial support, or interfere in local legal matters or arrests. *For more details, see Chapter 14.*

EMERGENCY/IMPORTANT CONTACT NUMBERS IN MEXICO

 Please consider putting some of these numbers in your phone prior to traveling to Mexico.

Emergency Numbers

- **Police (Policía Federal):** 911
- **Fire Department (Bomberos):** 911
- **Ambulance (Cruz Roja):** 911
- **Tourist Assistance (Asistencia Turística):** 078
- **National Guard (Guardia Nacional):** 088

Common Helpful Numbers

- **Directory Assistance (Información Telefónica):** 118
- **Mexican Consulate (for emergencies):**
- **U.S. Consulate in Mexico City:** +52 (55) 5080-2000
- **U.S. Consular Services (emergency):** +52 (55) 5080-2000 (for U.S. citizens)
- **National Poison Control Center (Centro Nacional de Envenenamiento):** 01 800 00 12 121

Healthcare Numbers

- **IMSS (Mexican Social Security Health Services):** 01 800 623 2323
- **Private Hospitals (varies by location):** Look up specific hospital numbers locally for emergency care.

Transportation

- **Taxi Service (varies by city):** Local numbers for taxis can be found in your area, or use ride-sharing apps like Uber or Didi.
- **Bus Information (Autobuses):** 060 (for intercity bus information)

Other Important Contacts

- **Weather Information (Servicio Meteorológico Nacional):** 070
- **Road Assistance (Asistencia Vial):** 072
- **Customs (Aduanas):** 01 800 4636 748

USEFUL SPANISH PHRASES

Greetings

HOLA – Hi/Hello

BUENOS DÍAS – Good Morning

BUENAS TARDES – Good Afternoon

BUENAS NOCHES – Good Night

ADIÓS – Goodbye

Magic Words

POR FAVOR – Please

GRACIAS – Thank you

DE NADA – You're welcome

¡SALUD! – Cheers!

PERDÓN/DISCULPA – Excuse me

SÍ/NO – Yes/no

Getting Around

¿DÓNDE ESTÁ EL BAÑO? – Where is the bathroom?

¿QUÉ HORA ES? – What time is it?

¿CÓMO LLEGO A...? – How do I get to...?

¿DÓNDE VA ESTE TREN/AUTOBÚS? – Where does this train/bus go?

RESTAURANTE – Restaurant

CUÁNTO CUESTA ESTO? – How much does this cost?

ESTACIÓN DE TREN/METROBÚS – Train/metro station

Communication

¿HABLAS INGLÉS? – Do you speak English?

NO ENTIENDO – I do not understand

NO HABLO ESPAÑOL – I don't speak Spanish

NO SÉ – I don't know

Emergency

¡AYUDA! – Help!

¡LLAMA A UNA AMBULANCIA! – Call an ambulance!

NECESITO UN MEDICO – I need a doctor

POLICÍA – Police

ESTOY PERDIDO/A – I'm lost

ES UNA EMERGENCIA – It's an emergency

GLOSSARY

ACQUITTAL: A jury verdict that a criminal defendant is not guilty, or the finding of a judge that the evidence cannot support a conviction.

ADVERSARY PROCEEDING: A lawsuit arising from a controversy that begins with filing a complaint.

AFFIDAVIT: A written statement made under oath.

APPEAL: A request made after a trial court has decided against one party in which the losing party asks a higher court to review the decision for legal error.

ARRAIGNMENT: A proceeding in which a criminal defendant is brought to court, told of the charges, and asked to plead guilty or not guilty.

BAIL: The temporary release of a person from jail when awaiting trial, on condition that a sum of money be lodged or deposited to guarantee an appearance in court.

BARRISTER: A lawyer admitted to plead at the Bar and who may try cases in superior court.

BURDEN OF PROOF: The duty to prove disputed facts.

CAUSE OF ACTION: A legal claim in a civil action.

COMPLAINT: A written statement that begins a civil lawsuit in which the plaintiff details the claims.

CONTRACT: An agreement between two or more persons to do something or to not do something.

CONVICTION: A judgment of guilt against a person charged with a crime.

CUSTOMS DUTY: A tariff or tax imposed on goods when transported across international borders.

COURT LIAISON: A person that coordinates with attorneys to perform administrative duties, such as scheduling witnesses, sharing information with law enforcement, and overseeing the reporting of cases to foreign embassies when applicable.

DAMAGES: Money that a defendant pays to a plaintiff in a civil case if the plaintiff wins.

DEFENDANT: 1) The individual against whom a civil claim is filed; 2) The individual against whom a criminal charge is filed.

FELONY: A serious crime, punishable by more than one year in prison.

MAGISTRATE: A judicial officer of a district court, who conducts initial proceedings in criminal cases, decides criminal misdemeanor cases, conducts many pretrial civil and criminal matters on behalf of district judges, and decides civil cases with the consent of the parties.

MISDEMEANOR: An offense punishable by one year or less in jail.

PLAINTIFF: A person or business that files a formal complaint with the court.

PLEA: In a criminal case, the answer of "guilty," "not guilty," or "no contest" in response to a criminal charge.

SOLICITOR: A lawyer who advises clients, represents them in lower court, and prepares cases for barristers to try in higher courts.

SOVEREIGN IMMUNITY: A legal doctrine by which the sovereign or the state (i.e. government) cannot commit a legal wrong, and thus, it is immune from criminal and civil liability and cannot be sued.

STATUTE: A written law passed by a legislative body.

STATUTE OF LIMITATIONS: A statute prescribing a period of limitation to bring certain types of legal actions. If the action is not brought within that time, the person or entity (in a criminal context) is permanently barred from suing in court.

SUBPOENA: A command, issued under court authority, for a witness to appear and to give testimony.

TESTIMONY: Evidence presented orally by witnesses.

VERDICT: The decision of a judge or jury in a case.

WARRANT: Court authorization to conduct a search or to make an arrest.

ACKNOWLEDGMENTS

This book series would never have seen the light of day without the able assistance of the following people:

Kathy Adams, my paralegal for over 22 years, who is the "Best" I've ever worked with during my entire legal career because of her amazing work ethic, organizational skills, and her ability to think outside of the box in unique and creative ways;

Ally Knez-Siddique, a professional writer, and one of my paralegals, whose eye for detail, according to her, is both a blessing and a curse;

Rosa Diaz Graham, my legal assistant who helped with research and word processing at the very beginning of this project;

Mindy Scarlett, my marketing and publishing "Guru"! Her creativity and vision have no boundaries!

ABOUT THE AUTHOR

Michael L. Moore practices in Orlando, Florida, the city where he spent his formative years. He credits the trauma of having his brother murdered when he was only 10 years old, as the catalyst that drew him into the practice of law.

Moore attended Florida State University, where he was a member of the FSU debate team. Upon graduating, he was awarded a full scholarship to attend the University of Tennessee College of Law, where he was elected President of the Student Bar Association. He further honed his advocacy and public speaking skills by participating in 'moot court' competitions.

After clerking at the Tennessee Attorney General's office while in law school, Moore moved back to Orlando, Florida, to work at the State Attorney's Office as a prosecutor, and where he was fortunate enough to meet the young lady that would eventually become his wife. Moore moved on to working for private law firms, both local and national, and eventually established his own law firm in 1999. He continues to make Orlando his home base.

It was the murder of a close friend and client in Jamaica that caused Moore to realize that books on laws in other countries were few and far between, and he was inspired to create Law of the Land Publishing. Moore launched Law of the Land Publishing to provide a series of guidebooks and a membership site for tourists and business travelers to stay up to date on the laws in each country they travel to, as well as having access to assistance if they run into legal issues.

"My vision is to educate people on what their legal rights are, and how they can access legal assistance, no matter where they have to travel to in the world," said Moore. "As Americans, we have a right to due process, but in some countries, you don't even have the right to access a square meal when incarcerated. My goal is to provide the information needed to stay out of trouble, as well as having access to assistance if trouble finds you."